How to Profit from the Next Bull Market

How to Profit from the Next Bull Market

ALAN DUSTIN

DUNDURN
TORONTO

Cover image: 123RF.com/ nerthuz
Printer: Webcom

Library and Archives Canada Cataloguing in Publication

Dustin, Alan, author
     How to profit from the next bull market / Alan Dustin.

Includes bibliographical references and index.
Issued in print and electronic formats.

ISBN 978-1-4597-3749-5 (softcover).--ISBN 978-1-4597-3750-1 (PDF).--ISBN 978-1-4597-3751-8 (EPUB)

1. Investments--Canada. 2. Portfolio management--Canada.
3. Stock exchanges--Canada. 4. Finance, Personal--Canada. 5. Bull markets. I. Title.

HG4521.D88 2017   332.6   C2016-907644-X
                                        C2016-907645-8

1   2   3   4   5   21   20   19   18   17

We acknowledge the support of the **Canada Council for the Arts** and the **Ontario Arts Council** for our publishing program. We also acknowledge the financial support of the **Government of Ontario**, through the **Ontario Book Publishing Tax Credit** and the **Ontario Media Development Corporation**, and the **Government of Canada**.

Care has been taken to trace the ownership of copyright material used in this book. The author and the publisher welcome any information enabling them to rectify any references or credits in subsequent editions.

— J. Kirk Howard, President

The publisher is not responsible for websites or their content unless they are owned by the publisher.

Printed and bound in Canada.

VISIT US AT

 dundurn.com | @dundurnpress |  dundurnpress | dundurnpress

Dundurn
3 Church Street, Suite 500
Toronto, Ontario, Canada
M5E 1M2

To Cathie

CONTENTS

PREFACE

In the mid-nineties, I had the opportunity to work at one of Canada's leading discount brokers. I began by working in the firm's call centre. It was a great place to start my career — the learning curve was exponential, and it created the foundation that I have built the rest of my career on.

If you're not familiar with how a call centre operates, here are the basics. A licensed representative answers incoming calls from clients as allotted through an automated system. No client is assigned to a particular representative, and, as a result, each rep is exposed to hundreds of investors, each with a different account size and level of sophistication.

As time went by, I started to recognize trends, and I also began to notice certain common characteristics shared by the larger accounts. What was it, I wondered, that contributed to these investors' success? What did they know that others did not? How were they different?

I observed that the accounts that were much larger than most all held similar stocks. Was I onto something? Some accounts were large, I knew, because of the success of an investor's outside business activities, such as employment. These investors were important, but I was more interested in the investors who had made their wealth as a result of their own investment expertise.

Later, as I developed my skills further, I earned a position in the options queue. It was now the late nineties, and the technology bubble was just gaining momentum. What I witnessed on the options desk was even more incredible than what I had seen on the equity desk. Millions of dollars were made and lost in those few years. A select few investors cashed out their millions before the bubble burst, but the vast majority ended up losing their gains and having to give everything back. What was it, I wondered, that these few successful investors possessed? How did they know when to realize their profits?

Eventually, I came to learn the answers to these questions. For more than twenty years I have had the pleasure of working as a full-service advisor with all sorts of clients, including some making their first investments and some with multi-million-dollar portfolios. Along the way I have learned as much from them as they have from me.

I have always worked to keep their money safe. That is one of the two most important principles I have learned about making money: First, you need to make sure that you don't lose it. Second, it is essential to take risks. These principles may sound contradictory, but they can work together.

Let me explain: I'm not talking about gambling; I'm referring to disciplined, measured, calculated risks that have a high probability of success. Calculated risks also have the potential for generating asymmetrical returns, which I'll discuss in more detail later in this book. These types of opportunities present themselves only once in every market cycle.

How does the average investor take advantage of these opportunities? This is the question I will attempt to answer in the following pages.

INTRODUCTION

This book is about how to make money. "So what?" you may think. "Money isn't everything." That's true. After all, what is money anyway? The dictionary defines it as a medium of exchange, a store of value, a unit of account. However, what money is by definition is not important. On the other hand, what money does for us is priceless. It allows us to acquire what we wish and to live meaningful lives. What does this mean for you? Do you want to go on a dream vacation, buy a home, purchase a luxury automobile, send your child to university, become debt- and mortgage-free, leave an inheritance, give to charity? When you are able to answer this question honestly, you will find your motivation to achieve your goals.

One of the best ways to increase your net worth is to invest. *How to Profit from the Next Bull Market* provides the keys to unlocking the secrets of successful stock market investing. Every investor knows that the bulk of investment returns are made in a bull market. Considering we are in the seventh year of a bull market, the second-longest bull market of the past one hundred years, we can conclude that most of the gains have already been made. Therefore, what is important at this stage of the cycle is capital preservation. There is a bear market approaching. I have identified a number of indicators throughout the book to prove my point and provided the steps you can take in order to protect yourself from the coming tsunami. Following these steps will help you accomplish two extremely important goals: it will prevent you from falling victim to another market crash, and, even better, it will position you properly to reap the rewards of the next bull market.

Even a person who does not have a great deal of investment experience recognizes that markets go through periods of ups and downs. There are four different types of markets: bull, bear, cycling, and congested. Besides being able to comingle with one another, they can exhibit a high degree of variability in factors such as length and amplitude. The potential combinations of these four basic types are endless. For example, a bull rally can take place in a bear market, or a bear market swing can occur in a cycling market.

The most common, the bull market, is an advancing market in which prices are going up for a sustained period of time. These types of markets can advance at a gradual pace or quickly, and they can last for several months or even years. There can be extremely strong bull markets, like the one leading up to the year 2000, or tepid bull markets, like the one we are currently experiencing. As the cycle matures they usually gain momentum, but they then become less sustainable and, therefore, more vulnerable to shifting course. Bull markets are among the most effective markets for the majority of investment strategies.

"Bear market" is the term used to describe a period in which stock prices are falling. Bear markets are the ones usually most feared by investors. They can be gradual and last for some time, but they are more known for panic price plunges that happen very quickly. They are usually the result of mass hysteria in the financial markets. The hysterical bear market is frequently violent and thankfully short lived. The stock market crashes of 1929 and 1987 were such bear panics.

Known as a trading range market, the cyclic market oscillates with shorter bull and bear movements within a trading range. Over time, the price action can be described as a wave pattern, moving up and down, confined within the boundaries of support and resistance levels. A cyclic market can also exist within a larger trend of a bull or bear market. A broad cycling market is the best market for traders.

The congested or consolidating market is typically characterized by the absence of a trend. A congested market consists of short-lived up-and-down fluctuations in price, typically referred to as whipsaw action. The congested market is the hardest market to make money in. It offers a limited amount of opportunity for short-term traders known as scalpers, who trade for small profits. However, even for them, these markets can be difficult to trade.

* * *

A few key differentiators set this investment book apart from others you may have read. In addition to providing you with essential investment knowledge, I show you how to correctly construct an investment portfolio that will keep you in control of your emotions, thereby avoiding costly mistakes. Secondly, I explain where to source valuable information and locate capital in order to research and fund your investment windfall. Most importantly, this book outlines a plan for buying a select group of equities at the right time — a plan that will show you how to profit from a bull market. This plan will provide you with the greatest likelihood of financial success.

You may have heard that the last decade has been named "the Lost Decade" — an appropriate name considering the poor investment returns the market delivered during that period. This may seem like something of a contradiction, since I've said that we are now in the seventh year of a bull market, but those investors who put their money in the markets in 2007 made their money back only very recently. The size of the market collapse in 2008–2009 was so large that it's taken a seven-year bull market to correct for it. Fortunately, the next decade doesn't have to be another disappointment — there is an excellent opportunity waiting just around the corner.

Before I get into discussing the strategies that can be used to take advantage of this opportunity, I think it's a good idea to get a clear picture of how things stand today for most people.

Chapter 1 begins with a high-level outline of the Canadian retirement landscape. What does the typical Canadian household look like financially? Only when we know where we are currently can we determine how to get to where we want to be financially tomorrow. For this, I provide an overview of what Canadians have at their disposal to plan for their financial future and ultimately provide for a comfortable retirement.

Chapter 2 outlines seven proven strategies for protecting your capital from the imminent bear market. Topics range from proper asset allocation to the correct use of derivatives for portfolio protection.

Chapter 3 provides a tutorial on basic financial math, and it will help you gain a greater appreciation for the power of compounding returns and an understanding of how you can use it to increase your net worth. You will learn how to maximize your registered retirement savings plans using a very conservative leverage strategy and why it is important to use all of your tax-free savings account contribution room. I also provide an introduction to the first of two powerful financial calculators.

Chapter 4 begins by identifying the greatest risk to retirement savings and offers solutions for managing it. No matter what stage of life you are in, these risk management solutions are the key to financial security. You will learn how to calculate whether you will have enough to retire wealthy. You'll also learn what age is the most advantageous to begin collecting the Canada Pension Plan and how to minimize the Old Age Security claw-back. I share my research on where to find the best funding sources for investments and retirement income. Finally, I grant you access to the only retirement calculator you will ever need.

Chapter 5 describes seven of the most important economic indicators and what they are currently signalling. You will learn which indicator Warren Buffett considers the most important and what it is telling us right now. You'll also learn who is responsible for our current monetary policy situation and why. Are Canadian housing prices overvalued? I will reveal the facts. Also, you will learn the one indicator that is very good at predicting the next recession.

Chapter 6 explores the predictive power of technical analysis and explains waves, patterns, and cycles. You will learn how one unassuming man has been able to predict market inflection points with uncanny accuracy and how pi can be used to predict market turning points. You'll also discover whether volatility can pinpoint the bottom of a bear market.

Chapter 7 will teach you how to read financial statements like a professional accountant. You'll learn how to find free research reports in the most unusual places, and you'll discover why high dividend–paying stocks may be riskier than you think. You'll learn what the biggest risk to the integrity of the financial system is and what the bond market can tell us about the equity markets. I explain why financial engineering has made the markets extremely dangerous. I end the chapter with some very interesting, rarely seen option repair strategies.

In Chapter 8 you'll learn how to identify when the market has reached the top. You'll also learn whether the U.S. presidential election cycle has been a good indicator for market corrections.

Chapter 9 identifies where we are in the market cycle. It shows you what techniques you need to know in order to attain the best execution prices, and it explains the do's and don'ts of leverage. You'll learn what the twenty most influential stocks are and why you should own them. Most importantly, I reveal the greatest secret to successfully investing in the stock market. Concluding the book, in Chapter 10 you can familiarize yourself with the trading rules of five of the most persuasive traders of our time.

1

THE CANADIAN RETIREMENT LANDSCAPE

Canadians are living longer due to healthier lifestyles and medical advances that have improved the treatment and control of the leading causes of death — cancer, cardiovascular disease, and stroke. As a result, our retirements are longer than they've ever been. Of course, we need to fund our retirements, and we can only do so with either the resources we have accumulated prior to retirement or the funds we have access to through government-assisted programs. If we have not prepared ourselves for our financial future properly, we have only a few options from which to choose: save more while we are working, spend less in retirement, or continue to work longer. Building wealth takes discipline, sacrifice, and hard work.

The alternative to doing so is clear when one considers that, according to a 2015 Fidelity Retirement Survey Report, the top five sources of retirement income for Canadians are the Canada Pension Plan (CPP) and Old Age Security (OAS) at 95 percent, registered retirement savings at 55 percent, non-registered savings at 45 percent, and defined benefit pensions at 35 percent. However, the maximum the combined CPP and OAS payouts are going to provide is approximately $15,000 in annual income, which likely won't be enough to cover most retirees' fixed expenses.

If that is true for your particular circumstances and you are serious about increasing your net worth before retiring, or if you simply want to be better informed, then read on! This book is geared toward helping you create wealth for your own financial independence.

The first secret to making money in the stock market is harnessing the power of compounding returns. For example, if you sell a stock short at the beginning of a bear market, the maximum profit potential is a 100 percent return, considering a stock has a lower bound of zero. However, if you buy a stock at the beginning of a bull market, the maximum profit is unlimited, potentially compounding your investment many times over.

When asked what their top financial concern is, about 60 percent of Canadians respond, "Not saving enough for retirement." Before you determine if you are saving enough, it's helpful to understand where most Canadians are positioned with respect to their own retirement. Let's start with a discussion of pensions.

SOURCES OF RETIREMENT INCOME

One thing is for sure: in the current environment of low interest rates, an aging population, and increasing longevity, pre-retirees need to save more if they plan to retire at the customary age of sixty-five. The market value of pension assets in Canada at the end of 2012 was $2.6 trillion. The smallest portion, $213 billion, or less than 10 percent, is held by the CPP and the QPP (Quebec Pension Plan). Employer-administered pension plans control the lion's share of pension assets, with $1.4 trillion, the majority of which is held in plans for public service workers. The remaining $928 billion is held by individuals in registered retirement savings plans (RRSPs). Despite constant media attention about all the unused contribution room in RRSPs and the frequent criticism of Canadians for their supposed inability to manage their finances for retirement, RRSPs have been the fastest growing of all pension assets. This reflects both increased contributions by Canadians and sufficient rates of return since 2009.

In 2012, just over six million Canadians were members of a registered pension plan. Such plans are divided into two types. Generally speaking, defined benefit plans are funded by the employer and defined contribution plans are contributed to by the employee. In the public service, about 80 percent of workers participate in defined benefit pension plans. This is a sharp contrast to the private sector. There, less than 30 percent of workers have registered pension plans. The "gold standard" defined benefit plans are enjoyed by an even smaller number of private sector workers — just over half of them, or 15 percent overall, are able to participate in defined benefit, employer-sponsored pension plans. The private sector has largely shifted to defined contribution plans as companies have come to understand how much more expensive and riskier defined benefit plans are. After the 2009 financial crisis, firms struggled to make up shortfalls in the funding of their defined benefit pension plans out of profits, precisely when funds were required for working capital. Of course, in the case of government-administered defined benefit plans, the risk is borne by taxpayers, so any deficits are paid for out of tax revenue.

Today, approximately six million Canadians are employed by small- and medium-sized businesses, which may not sponsor any kind of pension plan at all, and almost three million are self-employed. Private sector workers are more likely to change jobs and experience periods of unemployment, resulting in income fluctuations. These workers without defined benefit plans save for retirement using RRSPs, defined contribution plans, tax-free savings accounts (TFSAs), and non-registered (cash) accounts.

Since not all workers belong to an employer-administered pension plan, the self-employed and those who work for employers that don't offer pension plans must look after their own retirement savings schemes. Being self-employed or not belonging to an employer-administered pension plan does not necessarily condemn you to a life of poverty, but it does stack the odds against you. Nevertheless, Canadians have proven to be resilient, and they have adapted in the absence of an employer-administered pension by increasing the use of other savings vehicles like RRSPs and, more recently, TFSAs.

The shift away from defined benefit pension plans is often interpreted as creating a loss of security for pensioners, but this may not always be the case. Defined benefit plans can go bankrupt, whereas a defined contribution plan's payout is dependent solely on contributions and investment returns. Also, funding problems for defined benefit plans are not necessarily confined to the private sector. The Quebec Pension Plan is an example of a government-run plan that promises more benefits than current funding can support. This is mainly a result of its exposure to risky assets ahead of the 2009 financial crisis. However, Quebec's aging population is another problem for the plan. Eventually the QPP will require higher contribution rates or benefit cuts to avoid major changes.

The survival of an employer or the sufficiency of its pension assets is not the only source of uncertainty for pension plans. All such schemes are predicated on calculations about the likely average longevity of the plans' beneficiaries. Now, longevity risk assumes certain mortality rates, but given that Canadians are living longer due to our health care system and medical advancement, the old assumptions are no longer necessarily valid. Of course, any significant changes to these assumptions could spell trouble.

One way for pension plans to mitigate this risk is to shift from a defined benefit regime to a defined contribution one, which is what many of the plans sponsored by the private sector have been doing. Another way to adjust is to increase the age of eligibility. The Harper Conservatives had planned to change the rules governing Old Age Security payments, which Canadians are now entitled to begin receiving at the age of sixty-five, so that recipients would have to wait until the age of sixty-seven to begin receiving payments. That change was due to take effect starting in 2023, with full implementation by 2029. This hike in the age of eligibility was expected to save the government $11 billion per year. When the Liberals won the federal election in 2015, however, they overturned the roll-back. Good for retirees, bad for deficits.

Pensions and RRSPs are not the whole story, though. The majority of Canadians' personal assets are held outside pension plans. These assets are equally split between real estate and financial assets other than RRSPs. Most people's real estate assets don't extend any further than the principal residence; financial assets, on the other hand, can consist of cash deposits, securities, mutual funds, and other instruments. All of these assets provide potential sources of income for retirees. However, most current Canadian retirees, many of whom own their homes but lack other financial assets, have been reluctant to tap into assets like home equity as a source of retirement income. Younger Canadians seem to be more comfortable with the idea. It is one well worth considering, and I will be discussing the potential benefits of this strategy in more detail later.

THE RETIREMENT REVERSAL

Despite all of the retirement plans and other revenue streams available to potential retirees, in recent years there has been a marked reversal of the trend toward early retirement. Older Canadians are increasing their labour force participation and postponing retirement. According to the Fraser Institute, in 2013, one in four Canadians between sixty-five and sixty-nine years old was still working. Even people seventy and older are staying in the workforce in record numbers. Such seemingly small changes in the labour market have large implications for retirement income. The shift to continuing to work has several important implications for society. It supplies a pool of experienced productive workers to an economy facing possible labour shortages in the future, increases economic growth, eases the strain on pension benefits, and reduces the amount needed for retirement savings. The question must be asked, though: Is this reversal because of want or need?

In a study conducted by Statistics Canada in 2011, concerns were raised about the future adequacy of retirement incomes. The report expressed worry that up to a quarter of Canadians may face a drop of 25 percent in their standard of living when they retire over the next twenty to thirty years. This and other studies have formed the basis for provincial governments to push for an expanded CPP. The study attributed the expected drop in retirement incomes relative to working incomes to two main factors: a decline in the participation of employer-sponsored pensions and the increased failure of social security programs to keep pace with wage growth. One other factor contributing to lower retirement income, according to the report, was the fact that future retirees simply did not understand their own financial circumstances. According to the report, all too often Canadians did not finally become aware that they didn't have the assets to provide a comfortable retirement until it was too late.

There is, however, plenty of evidence to suggest otherwise. Canadians have demonstrated the ability to adapt their behaviour in response to their circumstances. They accept lower incomes so that they can retire early; they work longer when necessary; they save more to leave an inheritance; and they have a government support network in case of any health-related emergencies. The increasing financial literacy of the average Canadian is reflected in the rapid accumulation of assets and in the sharp decline in poverty among the elderly in recent years.

How Much Do You Need?

Enough with a general discussion, though! Let's get specific. Are Canadians saving enough for retirement? Let's look at some ballpark numbers. A simple way of calculating the assets required to provide an adequate annual income for a comfortable retirement is to divide the desired income by a conservative interest rate. (A more detailed method is explained in Chapter 3.) For example, $50,000 divided by 5 percent is $1 million. In other words, 5 percent of $1 million is $50,000.

This assumes principal is not being depleted. In reality, the average retiree would likely choose to spend some of the principal he or she has saved. In order to decide how long you may wish to ensure your retirement savings last, a mortality table can be used to calculate expected longevity based on age and gender. How long will your money last using both investment return and principal depletion? Here's an example: for a $50,000 annual income lasting twenty-five years and earning 5 percent, the initial amount required is actually $704,697. This does not factor in CPP, OAS, or any other pension income, so this lump sum could be reduced, but it does provide a good starting point. So it may be safe to say that $700,000 is a good target to aim for if you think $50,000 annually will maintain your standard of living. Next, using the downloadable financial calculator I've provided at www.thenextbullmarket.com, calculate the future value of your current savings plus any regular contributions, the time you have until retirement, and a conservative rate of return to achieve $700,000.

* * *

Now that you know how much you need to save to have a comfortable retirement, the question becomes, "How do I do that?" Evidence is clear that those who save for retirement using only defined contribution plans and RRSPs cannot realistically hope to accumulate even half the pension income of a career public service worker. Moreover, as income levels rise, the gap between the two widens further. So what can be done to give the private sector a better chance of enjoying the same benefits as the public sector?

A report published by the C.D. Howe Institute in 2008 recommended that changes be made to the tax rules with regard to investments and pension plans. One specific recommendation was that the self-employed be allowed to join individual pension plans. Some alternatives do exist for high-income earners, but the vast majority must rely on RRSPs. A major problem with this is that, while pension plans provide creditor protection, RRSPs do not. So, business owners, who often have a greater risk of financial loss than employees, have the additional worry of having their retirement savings seized by creditors in the event of bankruptcy.

As for employees, current tax rules stipulate that in order for a worker to participate in a pension plan, he or she must work for an employer that sponsors one. Private sector employers are not required to sponsor pension plans, however, and most do not. So, as with the self-employed, the only retirement savings option for most workers is RRSPs, with their limited savings room and lack of creditor protection.

Until now, pension reform has proven to be inequitable — despite the changes made, most private sector workers are still prevented from accumulating the pensions enjoyed by their public sector counterparts. According to a C.D. Howe Institute report on Canadian pensions, the solution is not to tamper with the successful public sector pension model or reduce pensions of public service workers. Rather, what is needed, according to the report, is a regulatory change so that something like the public sector model can become available in the private sector. This would give all Canadians the same opportunity to prepare for retirement, with or without the assistance of an employer.

Despite the difficulties of identifying precisely the number of Canadians who will retire with insufficient savings, what is certain is that there are considerable differences as to how well different classes of workers are prepared for retirement. We can make some generalizations. Public sector workers are well prepared, private sector workers with pensions are somewhat prepared, and those without such pensions are not. My job in writing this book is to level the playing field.

2

FIRST THINGS FIRST — HOW TO PROTECT YOUR PORTFOLIO RIGHT NOW

This chapter is dedicated to helping you preserve your capital. I discuss a number of strategies to protect your assets from a decline in value, and you may choose as many as you are comfortable with. A correction is coming, and I want you to be prepared or at least know what action to take when it does come. Hope is *not* an investment strategy.

CASH

Contrary to popular belief, holding cash is a useful investment strategy for periods of time such as market uncertainty or corrections. We have enjoyed a seven-year bull market, and that should suggest that caution is warranted. Anyone who is heavily weighted in equities at this point in the cycle is asking for trouble. Now is the time to be taking some equity profits off the table and allocating to cash. When I say "cash," I mean anything that is principal-guaranteed. This includes cash, money market instruments, treasury bills, redeemable guaranteed investment certificates (GICs), and any other liquid asset that has no risk to loss of principal. As a general rule it is always good to have some cash set aside in a portfolio for special situations. A typical portfolio in a "normal" market cycle should have 10 to 20 percent of its assets in cash. As a market moves higher, such as to where we are today, I recommend doubling that amount to 20 to 40 percent.

ASSET ALLOCATION

Asset allocation can be defined as the weighting of different asset classes held in an investment portfolio. The classes typically include cash, fixed income securities, and equity. Within those classes, the individual components vary widely. For example, a fixed income portfolio includes both government and corporate debt obligations. The "quality" or risk associated with any bond is the creditworthiness or assets that back that particular bond. A Greek government bond has more risk than a U.S. government bond. Likewise, a Microsoft corporate bond has less risk than a General Motors corporate bond. In the context of my discussion I refer only to Canadian and U.S. government bonds. There is no doubt that corporate bonds offer more attractive yields in today's market, but they will not protect you in a market correction.

As a general rule of thumb, your equity asset allocation should be one hundred minus your age. So at fifty years old your portfolio weighting would be 50 percent equity and 50 percent fixed income securities. At eighty you would be weighted 20 percent in equities and 80 percent in fixed income securities.

How much to shift as this bull market matures is a matter of personal preference, but I would suggest by 2017 you should be 100 percent in bonds and cash. In 2017, it will have been ten years since the start of the last market correction in 2007. If the markets haven't had a significant correction by then, I would be extremely shocked, considering we have been experiencing recessions at least once every ten years for the last century. Currently, at the time of writing, in the summer of 2016, I would be shifting 50 percent of equity holdings into bonds and cash every six months if you are currently in 100 percent equities today.

Having said that, I should stress that a select group of equities, otherwise known as "The Plan," will be the focus of the book in the coming chapters, since equity has proven to be an asset class that can significantly increase an investor's net worth in a reasonable period of time. Of course, investing in equities requires care — it is important that you buy the right securities at the right time. A wise person once told me that success is about being in the right place at the right time. Learning how to do this requires a lot of hard work and generally involves a number of learning experiences, otherwise known as mistakes. Since I have already done the hard work and experienced the setbacks, you should be able to benefit — if you follow The Plan.

Before I tackle equities, though, I think an introduction to some bond basics would be appropriate, considering they do have their place in a diversified portfolio, especially when preserving capital and reducing volatility is your primary objective.

Bond prices have an inverse relationship to interest rates. When interest rates go up, bond prices go down and vice versa. Think of a teeter totter. Interest rates have been at extremely low levels for an extended period of time now, and most would expect rates to start to go up at some point. Therefore, popular belief dictates that holding bonds in a rising interest rate environment is bad. You would be right if you thought so, but in my opinion it is better to hold an asset with the potential for a small loss (bonds) than to invest in an asset with the potential for a large loss (equities). I must qualify my statement by emphasizing that I am suggesting investing in short-term bonds.

Bonds have other characteristics that I believe are important to understand. For instance, their term to maturity affects their price sensitivity to interest rates. Short-term bonds, maturing in one to three years, have a lower sensitivity to interest rate moves than bonds maturing in twenty to thirty years. A long-term bond's price is highly sensitive to interest rate moves. This sensitivity to interest rate change is called "duration." For example, a short-term bond with a duration of two is expected to move up or down 2 percent in price for every corresponding 1 percent move in interest rates. Conversely, a twenty-year bond with a duration of nine is expected to move up or down 9 percent in price for every corresponding 1 percent move in interest rates up or down. Therefore, in a rising rate environment, long-term bonds should be avoided. Short-term bonds are your best choice. In a market correction, when rates are expected to be lowered (in order to provide stimulus), long-term bonds are your best choice.

Duration can be calculated for an individual bond or an entire bond portfolio with hundreds of holdings. To find out the duration of your bond holdings, call your financial advisor, who will be able to obtain this information for you.

Another bond market issue to be aware of is yield and yield-to-maturity disparity. Let me give you an example of what I mean by this. If you are looking at purchasing a bond mutual fund or exchange-traded fund (ETF), the fund may advertise a yield of 3.5 percent. However, it's possible that what you are really buying is a fund with a yield to maturity of 1 percent. In other words, although the current fund income stream could very well produce a yield of 3.5 percent, the bond portfolio was most likely purchased at a premium, so as the portfolio matures, the bonds will fall in price to par value, resulting in a capital loss.

To help you understand this scenario, let me give you an example. Assume you paid $102.50 for a one-year bond with a 3.5 percent coupon. Over the course of one year, you would collect 3.5 percent in interest, lose 2.5 percent in bond value, and end up with a net return of 1 percent.

Throughout modern history, one of the most effective means of wealth creation has been through the ownership of equities. More importantly, this process of wealth creation can be dramatically improved if equities are purchased at the right time. However, the reverse is also true. Holding a large percentage of equities at the wrong time can lead to overwhelming loss. Later in the book I will be discussing a group of twenty carefully selected equities that may offer you this same opportunity. But, for right now, your only concern should be keeping your money out of harm's way.

STOP-LOSS ORDERS

A stop-loss order is an order to sell a stock below its current market price. Wait a second — how is that possible? Let me explain. An investor who owns shares may place a stop-loss order below the current market price in order to establish a minimum sell price. The motivation in placing a stop-loss order is to preserve capital gains or predetermine a maximum loss the investor would be willing to sustain. With the exception of certain types of accounts, there is no cost associated with placing a stop-loss order — unless the transaction actually takes place.

Here's an example of how a trade involving a stop-loss order works: You buy a stock for $50 per share and the stock appreciates to $100. You believe the stock could appreciate further but don't want to risk losing more than 10 percent of the current $100 market price. What you could do is place a stop-loss order at $90.

The consequences of doing so would be twofold: it would give you the ability to participate in any further gains, should the shares continue to appreciate, and it would provide a disciplined sell target if the shares suddenly fell.

An investor must be mindful, however, that if the shares are later sold in the normal course of business, a stop-loss order must be closed if it has not expired. Otherwise, a sell would take place if the $90 share market price was reached. Considering the original shares would have previously been sold, this would effectively make your account short an equal number of shares.

A stop-loss order also has its limitations. When a share price falls steeply in the event of a significant material change, a stop-loss order becomes a market order below the stop-loss price. So it is possible for an order to be filled substantially lower than at your stop-loss price. To avoid this from happening, it is possible to place a stop-loss order with a limit. This would protect you from selling your shares at a price far below $90 in the previous example and create a price floor to which you would be willing to sell. As an example, you could place a stop-loss order to sell at $90 with a limit of $85. Therefore, if the shares you held dropped below $85, say to $80, the sell would not take place.

DERIVATIVES 101

Many investors find options too complex to understand, but I am here to help, so before you skip forward to the next chapter, let me encourage you to read on. I can explain these complex instruments in very easy-to-understand terms.

A derivative is an instrument whose value is derived from a change in price of an underlying asset. More specifically, an equity call or put option's value is determined by the change in price, up or down, of an underlying equity. Generally speaking, an investor who buys a call or sells a put is most likely interested in buying a stock. An investor who sells a call or buys a put is most likely interested in selling a stock. The difference in the four strategies is that buyers have the right, while sellers have the obligation. Buyers pay a premium for the right and sellers receive a premium for the obligation.

Derivatives have many uses, as we shall explore. One characteristic they have is the ability to control a large quantity of an underlying interest for little cost, otherwise known as leverage. This allows an investor to protect or "hedge" a large basket of stocks or a portfolio for a small percentage of the overall portfolio value.

Let's have a look at a couple of scenarios, starting with a call option.

Most people understand real estate, so I'll use the example of buying a house to explain a call option. Let's assume that you are buying a house from a builder whose completion date is in three years. The cost is $500,000 and the builder wants a 10 percent deposit, or $50,000. Everything goes according to plan and three years pass. The remaining deposit of $450,000 is due, but something else has happened in the meantime. The builder's houses are now selling for $600,000. You have two options at this point (no pun intended): you can purchase the house or you can sell it to someone else for $600,000.

So what just happened? Your equity has increased by $100,000 — a 20 percent return on $500,000. However, your option to purchase the house, or in this case your initial $50,000 deposit, has made a 200 percent return.

A call option works the same way. If a call is purchased and the underlying asset meaningfully appreciates in value, the call appreciates in price for a fraction of the cost of the underlying asset.

Put options have the same characteristics as insurance. Assume you purchase a new car and drive it off the lot. On the way home you get into an accident and your brand new car gets written off. The insurance company gives you the full value of the car and you are made whole again. The insurance company charged you a premium for the insurance, and they now assume the liability. This is conceptually how a put option works. A put option is purchased to protect the value of an asset against potential loss in value of that asset. If an underlying asset depreciates in value, the put option increases in price for a fraction of the cost of the underlying asset.

HEDGING USING OPTIONS

Hedging is a term used by risk market participants to describe a position taken that is opposite to or different from the primary position in order to mitigate or reduce that risk exposure. A bond manager wanting to reduce interest rate exposure would most likely use an interest rate swap. A global equity fund manager would use a currency swap to reduce currency risk. An investor concerned about an adverse move in equity prices would use an individual equity put option or a combination of call and put options. In the case of a portfolio or basket of stocks, index equity options may be the most appropriate hedging tool.

When interest rates were considerably higher, options were priced much differently. A call's value was greater than a put's since its intrinsic value incorporated the cost of carry (in this case, the cost of borrowing). At that time, a strategy known as a zero-cost collar could be used to hedge an individual stock or portfolio for no additional out-of-pocket expense. A collar is established by writing an out-of-the-money call (a call with a strike, or exercise, price that's higher than the stock's current price) to fund the purchase of an at-the-money put (a put whose strike price matches the stock's current price). This strategy effectively limits your upside profit while at the same time protecting the position from any downside loss. Since the drop in interest rates, the selling of a call will only finance a debit or bear put spread, which is the selling of a lower strike put along with the purchase of a higher strike put, and which does not fully protect the downside. As you will learn, however, this can still be used quite effectively to hedge a portfolio and is my preferred method of insurance.

Let's assume your portfolio is worth $450,000. How many puts would be required to hedge your portfolio? I'm assuming your portfolio's composition is somewhat similar to the broad index. In Canada, you could use the S&P TSX 60 large-cap stock ETF known as the XIU. Currently the S&P/TSX Composite is at 14,700 and the XIU is trading at $21.50. The 22 strike put (at-the-money) expiring in March 2018 is priced at $2.60. The 17 strike put expiring in March 2018 is priced at $0.90.

$$\$450{,}000 \div (22 \text{ strike} \times 100 \text{ multiplier}) = 204 \text{ puts}$$
$$204 \text{ puts} \times (2.60 \times 100) = \$53{,}040$$

A substantial 11.7 percent of your portfolio value! This means that an investor needs to spend $53,040 in put option contracts to protect a $450,000 portfolio.

Notice that I also quoted the 17 strike put expiring in March 2018. We could implement what is known as a bear put spread by buying the 22 puts and selling the 17 puts. This would reduce the cost of insurance but limit the downside protection to a 22.7 percent market correction ($22 - 17 \div 22$).

$$204 \text{ puts} \times (0.90 \times 100) = \$18{,}360$$

This reduces your insurance cost to $34,680 (($2.60 − 0.90) × 100 × 204), a less expensive 7.7 percent of the portfolio value, or about 3.8 percent per year, until March 2018.

Checking my strategy, if the market corrected by 22.7 percent, my portfolio value would fall by $102,500 ($450,000 × 22.7 percent). I could then sell my put insurance by closing the spread (204 × (22 − 17) × 100 = $102,000 — close enough!).

In 2009, the S&P TSX 60 or XIU dipped below $13, so in a similar market correction the bear put spread would *not* protect your portfolio losses completely. In other words, the market declined by 41 percent (from 22 to 13), but your portfolio insurance would have been limited to the lower put strike of 17, or 22.7 percent.

To lower my insurance cost even further, I could sell the 22 March 2018 strike call trading at $1.25, creating the last leg of the trade to form the collar. Therefore, my total out-of-pocket expense would be $9,180 (204 × (2.60 − 0.90 − 1.25) × 100), equal to 2 percent of the portfolio value.

With a U.S. broad-based portfolio, you could employ the same strategy using the S&P 500 SPY ETF. The SPY ETF is trading at $218.50 at the time of writing. Let's assume your U.S. portfolio is worth $650,000. The SPY 220 strike put expiring in March 2018 is priced at $21.15. The SPY 175 strike put expiring in March 2018 is priced at $7.45.

$$\$650,000 \div (220 \times 100) = 30 \text{ puts}$$

The SPY 220 March 2018 strike put is at $21.15

$$30 \times (\$21.15 \times 100) = \$63,450$$

This accounts for a reasonable 9.7 percent of your portfolio value. This means that an investor needs to spend $63,450 in put option contracts to protect a $650,000 portfolio.

The SPY 175 March 2018 strike put is at $7.45.

$$30 \text{ puts} \times (7.45 \times 100) = \$22,350$$

This reduces the insurance costs to $41,100 (30 × (21.15 − 7.45) × 100). This is a more reasonable 6.3 percent of your portfolio value, or about 3.1 percent per year until March 2018. If the market were to correct 20.5 percent, my portfolio would drop by $133,250 ($650,000 × 20.5 percent). The bear put spread hedge would be worth $135,000 (30 × (220 − 175) × 100).

In order to lower the cost of the insurance, I could sell an at-the-money call, just as in the previous example, to create a collar. The SPY 220 March 2018 call price is $14.90. Therefore, the total cost of the insurance would be a credit of $3,600 ($21.15 − $7.45 − $14.90 = −$1.20 × 30 × 100).

The SPY closed at 689 on March 6, 2009, so, needless to say, in an equally severe market correction there would still be another 60 percent (1,750 − 689 ÷ 1,750) on the downside. Ouch!

In theory, these option hedging strategies may seem practical, but some constraints do exist. For instance, many Canadian investors have much of their wealth in registered plans. Unfortunately, option trading is limited or restricted in these accounts, making hedging either impractical or impossible. Option trading is only permitted in non-registered margin accounts, so hedging a registered plan is likely done only through a non-registered account. If an investor has limited or no non-registered assets, then hedging may simply not be possible. There are, however, Canadian investments that are RRSP-eligible that use these strategies exclusively, as I explain near the end of this chapter.

INVERSE EXCHANGE-TRADED FUNDS

I liken exchange-traded funds, more commonly known as ETFs, to inexpensive mutual funds that trade on stock exchanges like individual equities. ETFs come in many varieties, from broad index baskets to more esoteric designs such as volatility, leveraged, or inverse market directional funds. Due to their low cost, in some cases as little as 15 basis points (or 15/100 of a percent), they have attracted a lot of investment dollars. This has usually been at the expense of poor-performing mutual funds with much higher fixed costs.

Inverse ETFs are designed to increase in value when the market drops. Therefore, it is possible to use them as a method of hedging your portfolio. However, some inverse exchange-traded funds come in single-, double-, and triple-levered units. They are re-priced daily and over time are subject to erosion. Due to this re-pricing, they should be used for only short periods, since time is their enemy.

The erosion of value is the result of basis risk. When a futures contract is used to hedge an underlying asset, basis is the difference in price between the spot (current) rate and a longer-dated futures contact. As a futures contract approaches expiration, the price converges on the spot rate. Therefore, the basis is lost as the contract expires or is "rolled" to a longer-dated futures contract, when the process starts all over again. Basis can also work in favour of a futures contract price, depending on the underlying asset or unique characteristics of the contract. Since we don't know when a correction is going to occur until we are in one, inverse ETFs should be used only when the timing of an event is non-essential — in other words, the event has already begun. Capturing profits during big market moves is key to holding for only a short period of time.

Some ETFs are financially engineered and use derivatives as opposed to the true underlying interest. This may lead to an additional problem: counter-party risk. Counter-party risk refers to the danger that the institution guaranteeing the other side of your transaction may suffer losses so significant that it is no longer able to meet its obligations. In the unlikely scenario of a catastrophic event, getting your trade settled by a bankrupt financial institution (counter-party) may leave you wondering why you didn't get paid despite being right. Some double- and triple-levered ETFs have been restricted from use at some brokerages. Speak with your financial advisor.

SHORTING STOCKS

Shorting stock is something that not a lot of retail investors understand, so a basic explanation of the practice may be helpful. In a sense, shorting stock is similar to renting a motor vehicle. If we rent a moving van, we require it for a specific period of time. We don't purchase a moving van if we only need one for a weekend in order to move across town. When we rent the van, however, we are responsible for bringing it back in the same condition and filling up the gas tank before dropping off the keys.

Investors, too, are also able to rent stock for a period of time. This is possible through a broker's lending desk. The stock can be rented at the current interest rate; the person renting it is responsible for returning the stock, paying the interest for the period for which the stock was rented, and paying any dividends to the owner.

Why would anyone want to do this? To make money, of course! So how does that happen?

When you short a stock, you sell it — even though you don't own it — and the proceeds are held in your margin account. If the stock drops in price, it can be bought back for less than the price it was sold for, and the difference is your profit. If the stock rises and you are forced to "cover" or buy back the stock at a higher price than what you shorted it for, the difference between that higher price and the original price represents your loss.

- Sell short 100 shares of Bre-X, Nortel, or Sino Forest at $10 on January 1
- Buy back 100 shares of Bre-X, Nortel, or Sino Forest at $2 on May 30
- Proceeds of short sale ($1,000) – purchase of shares to cover short sale ($200) = $800 profit

Why this strategy seems so risky to most investors is the belief that stocks have unlimited upside but can only fall to zero. This is true but highly unlikely. What is more likely is that a company will be acquired, causing its price to spike higher. Over a longer period of time, the shares may be called back by the owner or your profits may be eroded by the dividends you are responsible for. There are, however, very easy solutions to all of these risks.

First, only sell short-option eligible securities. In other words, only sell short stocks that have options that trade on them. This keeps your margin requirements to a minimum and allows you to buy a call option to guarantee your stock buyback price. Second, only sell short stocks that have no or a very small dividend yield. Finally, only sell short stocks with large public floats. This will serve two purposes: it will help you avoid a short squeeze (a sudden move up in the stock price that could force you to cover your position) and will mean there is ample stock to borrow from.

As an alternative to shorting stock and a way to avoid all of the inherent risks, buy deep in-the-money put LEAPS™ (long-term options). No margin risk, no dividend risk, and no risk of unlimited loss.

These are merely guidelines, and research and homework should be your first consideration in identifying the most profitable shorting opportunities. Since markets rise much more frequently and for much longer periods of time than they fall, it is fair to say that shorting stock is a difficult strategy, both fundamentally and emotionally. Not only do you need to be right when you choose a stock that is going against the uptrend of the market, but you also need to be patient — bull markets can last for extended periods of time. Because of these factors, I would only suggest shorting stock when a downtrend is confirmed and market psychology has turned decidedly bearish.

ALTERNATIVE STRATEGIES

Investors are looking for ways to smooth portfolio returns as the stock market displays increasing volatility and the bond market provides little in the way of yield or stability. Alternative strategies include a simple long/short approach, currency bets, a tactical-macro strategy, the use of managed futures, an event-driven strategy, a relative-value strategy, or a multi-strategy approach. A long/short strategy uses both long and short positions to earn investment returns. Sometimes pair trading is employed, in which the best-performing equity in a sector is bought while the worst performing equity in the sector is shorted. A tactical-macro strategy is a broad-based strategy in which sectors or geographic regions are over-weighted or under-weighted based on sentiment or expectations. Managed futures are investments that allow investors to gain exposure to the commodity markets. An event-driven strategy seeks to exploit opportunities that result from companies that are takeover candidates or are mispriced due to unexpected events. Unintended consequences may include factors such as governmental policy changes or large class-action lawsuits. Relative-value strategies include deep value (holding cheap stocks for a long time) or growth at a reasonable price. A multi-strategy approach can include many or all of the above strategies combined in one investment platform.

The first question you need to ask is what you want an alternative strategy to do. Are you worried about rising rates and want an alternative to fixed-income securities? Are you worried about volatility in the markets and want an alternative to traditional equity? Only a select few active fund managers in Canada make use of one or more of these strategies, specifically referring to the use of derivatives, if you wish to have a professional manage your money. If derivatives are used for their intended purpose, risk management, a professional manager can be fully invested in equities at any stage of a market cycle, even a correction, and risk little to no principal. I am familiar with just such a fund manager, whose performance was positive at the bottom of the 2008–2009 market correction. As derivatives become more transparent and accessible to retail investors who seek lower portfolio volatility, Canadians will become comfortable with them. They will also become attractive because of what they are designed to do: provide absolute returns.

Absolute return investments seek to deliver consistent, positive, absolute returns — whether markets are rising or falling. To do this, they invest in a wide variety of assets, such as equities, bonds, property, and cash. They also use advanced investment strategies, which are not always available to traditional investments, in order to seek additional returns or guard against market corrections. In implementing advanced investment strategies, absolute return investments often use derivatives, including futures, options, swaps, and forwards, whose values are based on an underlying asset, index, or reference rate.

In the past, derivatives have been associated with hedge funds whose high fees, minimum investment requirements, lack of transparency, and poor liquidity put off many retail investors. Moving forward, this may not be the case. Most conventional investments only reward investors when markets go up. Absolute return investments seek to deliver positive absolute returns over the medium to long term, whether markets rise or fall. Most do this by applying a range of low-correlation, diversified investment strategies that aim to generate positive returns whatever the market conditions. These strategies are devised so that if any individual strategy produces a negative return, positive returns from other strategies should be able to compensate.

Many pension funds in Canada now have the conviction to place large allocations of their assets in these investments. As more individual investors look to shelter assets from market volatility, these investments should grow in popularity very quickly. A few investment companies already have made their products available to retail investors in Canada. Speak to your financial advisor now.

3

HOW MUCH MONEY DO YOU NEED TO SAVE?

This question, of course, is very subjective. Only you know what your current and future lifestyle requirements are. I've seen it suggested that 70 percent of a person's pre-retirement income should provide a comparable standard of living. More recently, I've seen reports suggesting that early in retirement expenses may go down, but as we age expenses may increase due to additional health care costs.

We do know that one thing is for certain: over time, costs for products and services only move in one direction, and that is higher. Therefore, it is critical that our investments stay ahead of inflation and taxation.

MATH BASICS — THE RULE OF 72

Numbers have magical qualities, as we shall see. The Rule of 72 is a very easy way to determine either the rate of return required or the number of years it will take to double our money (or for it to lose half its value to inflation).

TABLE 3.1

The Rule of 72

	Rate of Return	Number of Years	
1.	12	6	72
2.	9	8	72
3.	8	9	72
4.	6	12	72
5.	4	18	72
6.	3	24	72
7.	2	36	72

From line 1 we can calculate that with a 12 percent rate of return we will double our money in six years. From line 4 we can determine that in twelve years we will double our money if we earn a 6 percent rate of return. From line 6 we discover that, assuming an inflation rate of 3 percent, the cost of goods and services will double in twenty-four years. In other words, our money will be worth only half of its current value in twenty-four years.

Now let's look at a specific example. Assuming that you are forty today, with a $300,000 portfolio, and you want to retire at sixty-five, how much money will you have? With a 6 percent rate of return, your portfolio would be worth $600,000 at age fifty-two, and at sixty-four it would be worth $1.2 million.

THE POWER OF COMPOUNDING

As I mentioned in Chapter 1, watching your investment growth compound from the beginning of a bull market is a beautiful thing! To understand how incredible compounding is, we need to explore some calculations that clearly demonstrate its power. Whether you are familiar with these equations or it is your first time seeing them is not important. What is important is that the concept of compounding is firmly imprinted on your psyche. Ultimately, it is your ability to compound your wealth that will lead you to your goal of financial freedom.

The formula to calculate future value is as follows:

$FV = PV(1 + i)^n$

Future Value = Present Value$(1 + \text{interest rate})^{\text{time}}$

By flipping this equation around, we can calculate what amount of money you need now (PV) or what interest rate or period of time is required in order to get to where you want to be in the future:

$$PV = \frac{FV}{(1 + i)^n}$$

For example, using the Rule of 72, the future value equation shows that you need an interest rate of 8 percent in order to double your money in nine years.

$1 \times (1 + 0.08)^9 = 1.999$

What if you invested your money at 5 percent for five years? What would be the percentage increase in your capital?

$1 \times (1 + 0.05)^5 = 1.27628 - 1$, or 27.6 percent

We can simplify the equation to $FV = (1.05)^5$

Proof: $(1.05) \times (1.05) \times (1.05) \times (1.05) \times (1.05) = 1.276281563$

If we *double* our money in ten years, what is the rate of return? This is what the equation looks like:

$2 = (1 + x)^{10}$ (using the Rule of 72, about 7.2 percent)

This calculation can be done on a financial calculator or in Excel very easily!

=POWER(2,1/10) = 1.071773463 − 1

If we *triple* our money in six years, what is the rate of return?

=POWER(3,1/6) = 1.200936955 (a little more than 20 percent, compounded annually!)

Proof: $(1.200936955)^6 = 3$

If we *octuple* our money in six years, what is the rate of return?

=POWER(8,1/6) = 1.414213562 (an enormous 41.4 percent compounded annually!)

These are not just arbitrary numbers I have chosen, as you will see later in the book; these are investment returns that have been achieved with equities. What's even more incredible is that these returns were made with companies that you are very familiar with. In some cases, we use their products and services every day.

One other powerful concept regarding compounding returns, with respect to reaching your retirement goals, is the risk necessary in order to achieve them. Contrary to popular belief, in short time periods (five years or less), an investor does not need to assume more risk in a portfolio in order to achieve greater returns. This is particularly true for a pre-retiree or someone investing in a seven-year bull market. I explore this risk in greater depth in Chapter 4. The following examples are representations of a balanced portfolio (A) and a growth portfolio (B), one much more volatile than the other. The end result may surprise you.

TABLE 3.2
Calendar Year Returns for Portfolios A and B over the Last Five Years

	1	2	3	4	5
A	5%	9%	8%	6%	7%
B	15%	−10%	−20%	35%	25%

Which would you prefer? Which investment had the highest return? Would you be comfortable with the volatility of Portfolio B?

TABLE 3.3

Calculation of Calendar Returns for
Portfolios A and B over the Last Five Years

	1	2	3	4	5	=PRODUCT(1:5)	=POWER(6,1/5)
A	1.05	1.09	1.08	1.06	1.07	1.40194	1.06991
B	1.15	0.90	0.80	1.35	1.25	1.39725	1.069

Both examples have the same return of 6.9 percent.

This example demonstrates that when making an investment with new money today, it may make more sense to invest conservatively and in lower-risk investments. The economist Harry Markowitz, best known for his modern portfolio theory, proved that constructing a well-diversified portfolio will significantly reduce risk without significantly diminishing returns. Remember what I said in Chapter 2 on asset allocation: we are in the final stages of the bull market, and adding to your fixed income and cash weightings as we head into 2017 is justified. "Swinging for the fences" at this stage of the cycle has no greater chance of success and carries with it significantly more risk. The asymmetrical returns I talk about later in the book are skewed disproportionately to the downside at this point of the market cycle. The asymmetrical returns we are waiting for are only attainable from the trough of the next bull market.

RETIREMENT ACCOUNTS

Countless books have been written on the benefits of contributing to an RRSP, so there is not much else I can say here that hasn't already been said.

When interest rates were much higher in the eighties and nineties, a common strategy was to have all interest-bearing investments inside an RRSP and growth investments outside. Doing this would allow you to receive interest payments tax-free and defer capital gains. More recently, due to the low-interest-rate environment, investors have been forced to seek higher returns with a greater portion of their assets. This in turn has resulted in increased exposure to risk assets, including equities, and U.S. equities in particular. The reason for this is twofold: U.S. dividends received inside RRSPs are non-taxable, and there has been no other alternative to risk-adjusted returns than investing in U.S. equities.

Canadian investors holding U.S. dividend-paying stocks are subject to a 15 percent non-resident withholding tax. Even with the tax treaty between Canada and the United States, withholding taxes can significantly reduce the after-tax yield on U.S. securities. A U.S. dividend yield of 3 percent is reduced to 2.55 percent. Therefore, in today's market, it may make more sense to hold high dividend–paying U.S. stocks inside an RRSP. If you have held U.S. equities in your RRSP account over the last few years, your return has also been enhanced by the positive carry (Canadian dollar depreciation). The only caveat is the currency conversion inside the RRSP. Make sure when buying and selling U.S. stocks inside an RRSP that the currency is not converted on each transaction, since the constant foreign exchange spread will reduce profits considerably. Canadian investors holding Canadian-domiciled stocks outside their RRSPs are entitled to receive the full dividend payment.

LEVERAGE YOUR RRSP

I have read a number of books recommending what to do with your RRSP contribution tax refund. Their recommendations include paying down your mortgage, plowing it back into your RRSP, and investing the proceeds in a non-registered account. These are all useful suggestions, but in my opinion the best strategy of all is to use these funds to apply leverage. Yes, the best use of such funds is to seek the most conservative leverage that an investor, even one with a low risk tolerance, can appreciate. Use the following formula to calculate the amount you are able to borrow so that the loan is completely paid off with your tax refund:

$$\frac{\text{Regular Contribution} \times \text{Marginal Tax Rate}}{1 - \text{Marginal Tax Rate}} = \text{Loan Amount}$$

Let's say, to keep the calculation simple, you contributed $10,000 to your RRSP and that you are in the 50 percent tax bracket. Based on this scenario, you could borrow an additional $10,000 for a total RRSP contribution of $20,000 (assuming available contribution room), and with the tax refund of $10,000 immediately pay off the loan. What you have accomplished through the use of this conservative leverage strategy is doubling your RRSP contribution. Many financial institutions will gladly provide you with an RRSP loan at a reasonable interest rate and defer your first loan payment for three months until you receive your tax refund, resulting in no out-of-pocket expense.

$$\frac{\$10,000 \times 0.50}{1 - 0.50} = \$10,000$$

TFSAs AND NON-REGISTERED ACCOUNTS

In 2009 the Conservative government launched a new retirement savings vehicle for Canadian residents called the tax-free savings account, or TFSA. The contribution limits have varied from year to year. Listed here are the annual contribution allowances since its inception. In the budget announcement in early 2015, the Conservatives increased the contribution amount to $10,000. However, after the Liberal election win, the amount was reduced back to $5,500 for 2016.

TABLE 3.4
TFSA Limits

1.	2009	$5,000
2.	2010	$5,000
3.	2011	$5,000
4.	2012	$5,000
5.	2013	$5,500
6.	2014	$5,500
7.	2015	$10,000
8.	2016	$5,500

As of 2016, the total contribution limit to date is $46,500. This dollar amount is now significant enough that, if invested for long-term growth, it can contribute to your net worth substantially, depending on your time horizon.

For those who have not taken advantage of this program, I can't stress enough how important it is that you do. Here's why. As this program gains popularity and allows investors to shelter gains tax-free, the government will continue to lose more revenue each year. Just as the personal lifetime capital gains exemption was eliminated, I believe that at some point the TFSA may face a similar fate as the government looks for ways to generate new sources of revenue. More recently, one of the TFSA founders released a statement commenting that the TFSA would result in billions in lost revenue to government coffers and that contribution limits should be reassessed.

A friend of mine suggested that the name "tax-free savings account" is really a misnomer. A more appropriate name would have been the "tax-free investment account." Let me explain. Even though interest income and Canadian dividends are received tax-free in a TFSA, these gains don't represent the potential of long-term capital growth. Further, U.S. dividends received in a TFSA are still subject to the 15 percent withholding tax, because a TFSA does not offer the same status as an RRSP or RRIF.

A TFSA holder's main objective should be capital appreciation, and that is achieved only by holding good-quality equities over the long term. Currently, as money is withdrawn from a TFSA, the proceeds are not added to income like a company pension or RRSP or RRIF payouts. As a result, it will not cause government benefits such as Old Age Security to be clawed back. If you have contribution room and are holding assets that meet the criteria of long-term capital appreciation in a non-registered account, you may contribute in-kind into a TFSA. The asset will be deemed to have been sold at fair market value, but any growth inside the TFSA will then be tax-free.

Non-registered accounts, otherwise known as a cash or margin accounts, are another investment vehicle for achieving financial independence. These accounts do not offer the benefits of being tax sheltered like an RRSP or a TFSA, but they allow cash to be deposited or withdrawn easily. Interest and dividend income are subject to taxation each calendar year when received. Similarly, capital gains tax is triggered upon disposition of assets. These accounts are typically held at financial institutions where cash or direct investments can be purchased and held. They can be used for leveraging, which I will explore in much greater detail in Chapter 9. In addition, under normal circumstances, they should be held jointly with spouses in order to avoid unwarranted taxes. Speak to a tax professional for further information.

GOAL CALCULATOR

Calculating what you need to save for a specific goal is effortless. Comparisons and illustrations can be created on any amount of systematic investment, rate of return, or period of time. For instance, let's assume that you're forty years old and would like to retire with $700,000 at sixty-five. You have savings of $100,000 between your RRSP and TFSA and are currently contributing $500 comfortably each month. What rate of return do you require to meet your goal of $700,000?

The answer is 5.50 percent. I have sketched out the calculation in Table 3.5, and the graph that follows shows the growth in savings visually.

FIGURE 3.1
Growth in Savings

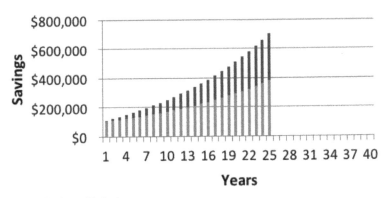

■ Growth of Monthly Savings

▩ Growth of Initial Investment

TABLE 3.5
Growth in Savings Calculator

Initial Investment:	$100,000
Monthly Contribution:	$500
Rate of Return:	5.50%
Number of Years:	25
Total Initial Growth:	$381,339.23
Total Monthly Savings:	$321,018.72
Growth Savings:	$702,357.95

Years	Growth of Initial Investment	Growth of Monthly Savings	Total Savings
1	$105,500	$6,154	$111,654
2	$111,303	$12,654	$123,957
3	$117,424	$19,522	$136,946
4	$123,882	$26,776	$150,659
5	$130,696	$34,440	$165,136
6	$137,884	$42,537	$180,421
7	$145,468	$51,090	$196,558
8	$153,469	$60,125	$213,594
9	$161,909	$69,670	$231,580
10	$170,814	$79,754	$250,568
11	$180,209	$90,406	$270,615
12	$190,121	$101,659	$291,780
13	$200,577	$113,547	$314,125
14	$211,609	$126,106	$337,715
15	$223,248	$139,373	$362,620
16	$235,526	$153,388	$388,914
17	$248,480	$168,194	$416,674
18	$262,147	$183,835	$445,982
19	$276,565	$200,358	$476,923
20	$291,776	$217,814	$509,589

Years	Growth of Initial Investment	Growth of Monthly Savings	Total Savings
21	$307,823	$236,254	$544,077
22	$324,754	$255,734	$580,488
23	$342,615	$276,313	$618,928
24	$361,459	$298,053	$659,512
25	$381,339	$321,019	$702,358

For more details on how to calculate the growth in your own savings, go to www.thenextbullmarket.com to download your free copy in Excel.

4

HOW MUCH MONEY DO YOU NEED TO RETIRE COMFORTABLY?

As I mentioned in the last chapter, the general rule for post-retirement income has been approximately 70 percent of pre-retirement income. More recently, many experts believe that as we age, we require more income due to an increase in optional out-of-pocket health care costs. These additional treatments, therapies, and medications may not be covered under normal government or private benefit plans.

Let's assume that $50,000 is your magic number. At a discount rate of 5 percent, that would require you to have a $1 million nest egg. As you age, you could chip into the principal to make up any shortfall from investment return alone. However, factors like being too generous to loved ones could deplete your nest egg quicker. Additionally, because of health care, diet, and exercise, you risk living much longer than you anticipated. This is a good thing, of course, but it also means that you need to be a bit more mindful of your spending habits. The key to finding an appropriate answer is balance. On one hand, we should be able to enjoy retirement and spend some of our hard-earned money, certainly while we are still in good health. On the other hand, we should not be irresponsible and risk running out of dough too soon. The best way to ensure what your retirement cash flow needs will be is to prepare a personal retirement budget. Download your free retirement budget worksheet from www.thenextbullmarket.com.

Rules of Thumb — How to Determine If You Are Wealthy

Who is wealthier, a forty-year-old man earning $250,000 per year or a forty-five-year-old woman earning $100,000?

Wealth is subjective and has many different interpretations. It is not only a function of cash flow or the number of possessions you have. Wealth is a measure of net worth. It is a calculation based on how much you are worth when you compare the value of your assets to the scope of your liabilities.

According to Thomas Stanley, author of *The Millionaire Next Door*, the simple rule of thumb for determining if someone is wealthy is to multiply their age by their gross income from all sources except inheritances. Divide by ten. This, less any inherited wealth, is what your net worth should be. Another simple rule for being well positioned says you should be worth twice the level of wealth expected.

Is this forty-year-old man, who is living paycheque to paycheque with zero assets, wealthy? Absolutely not. Is this forty-five-year-old woman, who owns a $400,000 condominium mortgage-free and has $100,000 in investment savings, wealthy? According to Stanley's formula, she isn't yet, but she is well on her way:

$$\$100,000 \times 45 = \$4,500,000 \div 10 \text{ is } \$450,000$$

The condo and savings are valued at $500,000. Therefore, not having a million dollars does not automatically make one less fortunate.

However, for a sixty-year-old earning $400,000 per year with $1.5 million in net worth, the complete opposite is true. Is this person a millionaire? Yes. Is this person wealthy? Not even close.

So, how do you determine if you will be wealthy enough to retire? My retirement calculator will help you to figure that out.

Retirement Calculator

This is by far the most powerful calculator I have to offer in my tool box. The reason is twofold. It is extremely easy to use, and it answers the question that weighs on everyone's mind: Do I have enough money to retire comfortably? Consider the example illustrated in the graph and table that follow. You have $1 million and need to withdraw a $60,000 income per year. If possible, you would also like to leave a $250,000 inheritance to loved ones. Can it be done assuming a 5 percent rate of return? Simply input the data into the calculator, and presto! You have approximately thirty-two years until your funds are depleted. Go to www.thenextbull market.com to download your free copy in Excel.

FIGURE 4.1
Retirement Income Projection

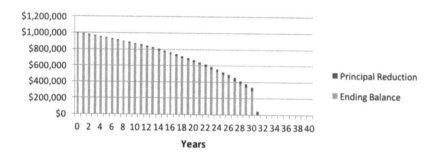

TABLE 4.1
Retirement Savings Calculator

Rate of Return:	5.0%
Annual Income:	$60,000
Retirement Savings:	$1,000,000
Estate Value:	$250,000
Monthly Rate:	0.417%
Monthly Income:	$5,000
Years After Retirement:	32

Year	Beginning Balance	Gain/Loss	Annual Income	Principal Reduction	Ending Balance
0	$1,000,000	$50,000	$60,000	$10,000	$990,000
1	$990,000	$49,500	$60,000	$10,500	$979,500

Year	Beginning Balance	Gain/Loss	Annual Income	Principal Reduction	Ending Balance
2	$979,500	$48,975	$60,000	$11,025	$968,475
3	$968,475	$48,424	$60,000	$11,576	$956,899
4	$956,899	$47,845	$60,000	$12,155	$944,744
5	$944,744	$47,237	$60,000	$12,763	$931,981
6	$931,981	$46,599	$60,000	$13,401	$918,580
7	$918,580	$45,929	$60,000	$14,071	$904,509
8	$904,509	$45,225	$60,000	$14,775	$889,734
9	$889,734	$44,487	$60,000	$15,513	$874,221
10	$874,221	$43,711	$60,000	$16,289	$857,932
11	$857,932	$42,897	$60,000	$17,103	$840,829
12	$840,829	$42,041	$60,000	$17,959	$822,870
13	$822,870	$41,144	$60,000	$18,856	$804,014
14	$804,014	$40,201	$60,000	$19,799	$784,214
15	$784,214	$39,211	$60,000	$20,789	$763,425
16	$763,425	$38,171	$60,000	$21,829	$741,596
17	$741,596	$37,080	$60,000	$22,920	$718,676
18	$718,676	$35,934	$60,000	$24,066	$694,610
19	$694,610	$34,730	$60,000	$25,270	$669,340
20	$669,340	$33,467	$60,000	$26,533	$642,807
21	$642,807	$32,140	$60,000	$27,860	$614,948
22	$614,948	$30,747	$60,000	$29,253	$585,695
23	$585,695	$29,285	$60,000	$30,715	$554,980
24	$554,980	$27,749	$60,000	$32,251	$522,729
25	$522,729	$26,136	$60,000	$33,864	$488,865
26	$488,865	$24,443	$60,000	$35,557	$453,309
27	$453,309	$22,665	$60,000	$37,335	$415,974
28	$415,974	$20,799	$60,000	$39,201	$376,773
29	$376,773	$18,839	$60,000	$41,161	$335,612
30	$335,612	$16,781	$60,000	$43,219	$292,392
31	$292,392	$14,620	$60,000	$45,380	$0

THE GREATEST RISK TO RETIREMENT

There are two essential components necessary in order to achieve investment success: investing at the right time and patience. Once you're retired, time becomes your enemy. Why? Basically, if you lose a portion of your portfolio value because of a market correction, you may not have enough time to recover. This unfortunate state of affairs is magnified should you also be withdrawing an income from your savings. This risk is known as sequence-of-return risk. In other words, if you are drawing an income from a pool of assets that are depreciating in value, those assets will be depleted at a faster rate. Further, without enough time to wait for a recovery before continuing to draw the income, you may deplete your money a lot sooner than planned.

Anyone who has a mortgage understands the opposite of this principle. Making your regular mortgage payment reduces your amortization on a known trajectory. However, making additional lump sum payments shaves years off your mortgage balance.

So how do you avoid becoming a victim of this unfortunate circumstance if you're approaching retirement or already there? One way to avoid getting stung is proper asset allocation. Especially in the later years of a bull market, it is important to have your portfolio structured to preserve capital. Reduce your equity exposure and increase the correct bond allocation. Refer back to Chapter 2 if you require a refresher.

The second way is holding cash. As I have already mentioned, in a volatile market holding cash is an appropriate investment decision, despite what the experts say. After all, it is only temporary. There will inevitably be an opportunity just around the corner to buy excellent companies at discount prices.

To prove my point, I have provided two portfolios that are identical in every respect except for one difference: the sequence of returns. Portfolio A initially experiences poor market performance, whereas Portfolio B initially experiences good market performance. What is important is that the outcomes are dramatically different. Where Portfolio A starts with a negative 15 percent return, Portfolio B ends with it. The assumption is that both portfolios are producing a return of 6 percent and providing an income of $5,000 per year. As a result of unfavourable market conditions, Portfolio A is depleted in less than twenty years. On the other hand, Portfolio B more than doubles its original value in twenty-five years.

Which would you prefer? Is it time to review your portfolio? What is the market telling us right now? In my opinion, and that of George Soros,

Bill Gross, Carl Icahn, Jeffrey Gundlach, and many others, the stock market is vulnerable and may soon experience a major correction.

TABLE 4.2
A Comparison of Portfolio Growth

Year	Portfolio A (CAGR* 6%)		Portfolio B (CAGR 6%)	
	Return	Balance	Return	Balance
0		$100,000		$100,000
1	−15%	$80,750	22%	$115,900
2	−4%	$72,720	8%	$119,772
3	−10%	$60,948	30%	$149,204
4	8%	$60,424	7%	$154,298
5	12%	$62,075	18%	$176,171
6	10%	$62,782	9%	$186,577
7	−7%	$53,737	28%	$232,418
8	4%	$50,687	14%	$259,257
9	−12%	$40,204	−9%	$231,374
10	13%	$39,781	16%	$262,594
11	7%	$37,216	−6%	$242,138
12	−10%	$28,994	17%	$277,452
13	19%	$28,553	19%	$324,217
14	17%	$27,557	−10%	$287,296
15	−6%	$21,204	7%	$302,056
16	16%	$18,796	13%	$335,674
17	−9%	$12,555	−12%	$290,993
18	14%	$8,612	4%	$297,433
19	28%	$4,624	−7%	$271,962
20	9%	$0	10%	$293,658
21	18%	$0	12%	$323,297
22	7%	$0	8%	$343,761
23	30%	$0	−10%	$304,885
24	8%	$0	−4%	$287,890
25	22%	$0	−15%	$240,456

*Compound annual growth rate
Source: Fidelity Investments

Looking at this table brings to mind another risk that is extremely relevant at this time: longevity risk. In the previous example, as the owner of Portfolio A you could come to the realization that there is a good possibility you may outlive your savings. As improved health care and medical treatment increase your odds of living longer, you would have to take steps to ensure that you didn't burn through all of your cash before the end of your life. This can only be achieved through proper planning and proactive behaviour. That is why it is extremely important to find a qualified financial advisor sooner rather than later if you don't have the skill set to properly manage your financial affairs. You have to be completely honest with yourself. Your future depends on it!

INSURANCE — RISK MANAGEMENT 101

Planning for the future must account for all types of known and unforeseen events. As a consequence, an essential part of becoming financially secure is having protection from either catastrophic losses or exorbitant tax liabilities. Therefore, insurance in the form of risk management does have a role to play. I have outlined a number of scenarios in which insurance in some form can make the difference between a manageable outcome, regardless of what life may thrust upon you, and a financial and emotional disaster.

Whether you travel out of the province you live in or out of the country, a part of your planning for any trip should be purchasing travel insurance. Today, this can be done through any financial institution over the phone in a matter of minutes. Further, depending on your age, insurance is very affordable and may not even require a medical exam. The benefits of travel insurance far outweigh the costs. If you do require medical treatment while travelling abroad, the costs could be devastating.

For example, while travelling on a personal vacation in the Caribbean I caught a stomach bug that required hospitalization, medication, and treatment. The medical bill for the overnight stay while recovering was approximately $5,000. Although that wouldn't have financially ruined me if I hadn't purchased insurance, it would have been a lot more than I wanted to pay for a horrible vacation.

Another example: I had husband-and-wife clients who travelled to the United States, as many of us do, to escape the winter months, and while there the wife had a massive heart attack. The medical bills alone were in the hundreds of thousands of dollars. This would have been financially devastating for them had they not had travel insurance.

The bottom line is this: if you are planning to travel, the first item on your "to do" list should be purchasing inexpensive travel insurance.

Even if you're not travelling, critical illness insurance has a part in risk management as well. Those who are not covered through employment or do not want to be a financial burden on family may choose to acquire insurance in order to protect personal financial assets in the event of a serious illness. Illnesses that qualify for coverage typically include cancer or heart-related ailments. The odds are quite high that at some point in our lives we will suffer a serious health concern. The benefit of critical illness insurance is that the payout is a one-time lump sum and is received tax-free.

Of course, there are many additional non-critical medical costs that most people face, particularly as they age. Some individuals do not have a family support network, may not have coverage through their employer, or simply want to ensure their own families' well-being and security. In these instances, there is a wide range of products to assist with health expenses above the provincial minimums. Health insurance can be purchased by individuals who want medical, dental, and vision coverage for themselves and their families. More extensive benefit packages may also include chiropractic and physiotherapy treatments. Planning for post-retirement introduces the need to consider a long-term-care policy in order to live in dignity as we grow older.

Insurance needn't be restricted to medical issues, though — it has its uses in helping to manage the financial stresses of daily life. As newly married couples start to build a life together, for instance, they typically incur a number of liabilities that are a part of life. These include large debts, such as a mortgage. Parenthood also brings with it additional costs. At this stage, cash flow is usually one of the biggest constraints. An ideal solution for these major liabilities is inexpensive term insurance to cover the outstanding debt and bridge the income gap.

For those in the fortunate position of having significantly funded registered accounts or substantial real estate assets, the government is patiently waiting to collect its share. With respect to your registered accounts, such as an RRSP or RRIF, the tax will be almost half the dollar value. Real estate will be taxed more favourably as a capital gain. A term insurance policy could be used to mitigate the liability and leave your estate whole. A few more expenses that should also be taken into consideration are funeral expenses, a family cottage, and a taxable investment portfolio that will be deemed to be sold at fair market value.

One of today's challenges for risk-averse investors is earning a good income that is tax efficient as well as guaranteed. With GIC rates where they are today, it just doesn't make sense to invest in GICs. A better alternative may be an insured annuity, which is designed to provide you with a tax-efficient stream of income for a set period or life. If the annuity is for life, upon your passing it will provide your beneficiaries with the capital you initially placed in the policy. Since each insurance carrier has its own strengths and weaknesses in terms of its product shelf, it is a good idea to shop around for the best available terms. An insurance agent who works through a managing general agent (MGA) will be able to save you the trouble, since they represent multiple carriers and will be able to do the leg work. When working with an agent, it is always a good idea to obtain three quotes from different carriers and choose from the best one.

Another possible alternative to a guaranteed income stream is a segregated fund. Segregated funds are mutual funds or exchange-traded funds in an insurance wrapper, so a portion of their values may be linked to equities. This being the case, the timing of the purchase should be the largest consideration, since it determines the value of the corresponding equity component. However, depending on the product chosen, a 100 percent death benefit is most likely embedded in the contract. Many of these products contain the phrase "Guaranteed Minimum Withdrawal Benefit" (GMWB) in their names and have a 4.5 to 5 percent annual payout.

For those who own and operate successful businesses, there are an abundance of products and services designed to benefit you in every aspect of your financial affairs, including business, personal, and a combination of the two. On the business side, you have products to safeguard business succession or provide disability income in case of injury. On the personal side, insurance may be used to preserve your estate value or provide equalization for two or more beneficiaries.

Regarding beneficiaries, not all are created equal. Although we do our best to raise children who are contributing members of society, some may not be very financially responsible. If you are concerned about your beneficiaries spending their inheritance soon after your passing, there is an insurance product for that, as well, that pays out an income for as long as you choose.

Philanthropy is one of the qualities that set Canadians apart from residents of other nations. If it is your intention to donate a gift to a charity while living or after passing, it is quite possible an insurance product exists that may provide for both a greater gift and preferential tax benefits.

CPP AND OAS

Examining CPP and OAS on a deeper level will help you understand what the best course of action is to maximize benefits. The maximum CPP allowance for a Canadian pensioner as of March 2016 was $1,092.50 per month. However, do not expect the maximum. In fact, the average CPP payment is currently $629.33. The best way to find out how much you qualify for is to contact Service Canada at 1-800-277-9914 and ask for your CPP Statement of Contributions.

Planning your retirement needs and income requires some understanding of how much you will get from CPP and OAS. Another consideration to keep in mind is that, if your income is above a certain threshold, OAS benefits will be clawed back at a rate of $15 for every additional $100 of income. Therefore, it is important to plan to receive income in the most tax-efficient manner in order to maximize your OAS benefit. The OAS repayment range in 2016 is $73,756 to $119,398. That is, anyone earning an income over $119,398 automatically loses all of their OAS benefit.

One of the most frequent questions I hear from investors is when to start taking CPP. Of course, this is a matter of necessity, first of all. However, looking at this question on an empirical basis, what makes the most sense? According to the current guidelines, CPP can be taken as early as your sixtieth birthday, with a 7.2 percent reduction for each year before sixty-five. Therefore, at sixty you would be entitled to receive CPP at a 36 percent reduction. The big question then becomes, "If I decide to receive CPP at sixty, at what age would the payout be equivalent to waiting until sixty-five?" That number happens to be fourteen years. In other words, at age seventy-three it makes no difference in dollars if you had chosen to collect early or waited until sixty-five. After that, it begins to work against you.

TABLE 4.3
Collecting CPP at 60 versus 65

Age	CPP at 60	CPP at 65
60	$4,833	
61	$9,667	
62	$14,500	
63	$19,333	
64	$24,166	
65	$29,000	$7,552
66	$33,833	$15,104
67	$38,666	$22,656
68	$43,499	$30,208
69	$48,333	$37,760
70	$53,166	$45,312
71	$57,999	$52,864
72	$62,832	$60,416
73	$67,666	$67,968
74	$72,499	$75,520
75	$77,332	$83,072
76	$82,165	$90,624
77	$86,999	$98,175
78	$91,832	$105,727
79	$96,665	$113,279
80	$101,498	$120,831

Certain circumstances would make the decision to collect early more beneficial, such as the quality of life you have. If you are not in good health, if you feel that you would make better use of the money earlier, or if you don't need the money but want to begin to build an inheritance for loved ones, then the decision to collect early would make sense. For these reasons, I think it is safe to say that starting at sixty is the popular choice. Of course, some want to collect as soon as possible because they believe that government benefits may be at risk in the future.

For others who may wish to defer CPP benefits, waiting until after sixty-five increases your payout by 8.4 percent for each year up until seventy. At seventy, your benefit would be 42 percent greater than if you had begun at sixty-five.

If you would like to see how different streams of income are taxed and which are most beneficial on an after-tax basis, go to the website https://simpletax.ca/calculator and compare them using any hypothetical scenario.

There is a confluence of factors affecting a retiree's level of income and ability to maintain the same standard of living every year. The Liberal government has promised no change to CPP and OAS benefits in recent election promises. However, the running of larger deficits and ballooning federal debt may challenge this entitlement sooner or later. Low interest rates have forced savers to accept lower fixed returns. Cutbacks to social programs force more Canadian to pay out of pocket. So what is a retiree to do to bridge the gap? Luckily for some, there are a few options.

Sources of Income

Regardless of your age, if you are a homeowner and have equity in your home, it is essential that you apply for a home equity line of credit (HELOC). The best time to do this is when you *do not* need the money. There are considerable fees involved in arranging a HELOC, but the benefits far outweigh the costs. When applying for a line of credit, you will need to provide income verification and cover the fees for an appraisal and independent legal advice, which will cost between $700 and $1,000. What you will get in return is peace of mind. Having access to an affordable, low-interest, open line of credit can offer many benefits. They include provision of an emergency fund for covering unexpected costs; the option of replacing high-interest credit card debt with a low-interest loan; the possibility of funding an RRSP loan; and the provision of funds for a vehicle purchase, investment in equities or an income property, home repairs or renovations, and vacations or a vacation property. The list is endless. If you haven't applied for one already, do it now!

In recent years, low interest rates have caused many retirees living on a fixed income to dip further into their savings than originally planned. Many adult children have had difficulty finding meaningful employment, and aging parents have had to support them after graduation, putting additional strain on many Canadian families' income. Whatever the reason, it seems that we are in more need of cash now than ever before. For many Canadian homeowners, the prospect of using their home as a source of cash flow has led them to consider a reverse mortgage. Before making a decision, be sure you also consider other possibilities, such as using a conventional mortgage or the equity in your home to secure a home equity line of credit. Another option to consider is selling your home, in favour of downsizing or renting, since it would provide an immediate lump sum you could use to purchase an annuity or provide a regular income stream. If you are opposed to giving up your much-loved home, you have other options, like taking in a renter or selling your home to one of your children and maintaining occupancy.

Currently, only one vendor in Canada issues reverse mortgages. The CHIP Reverse Mortgage is offered by HomEquity Bank with both variable and fixed-rate options. The variable term offers a six-month introductory rate of 3.99 percent, with $1,495 in closing and administration costs. Thereafter, the variable rate is 4.95 percent. The five-year, fixed-term rate is 5.49 percent, with $995 in closing and administration costs. The applicant is responsible for the appraisal and independent legal advice in both instances, which costs between $700 and $1,000. To qualify for a reverse mortgage, you do not need to provide credit, income, or medical history. You need to be at least fifty-five years of age, and you can borrow up to 55 percent of the value of your home. The income is non-taxable and will not affect government benefits. Over time, there is also a guarantee that your borrowing limit will never exceed the value of your home. The homeowner is never required to make any payments, and the full amount is due when you sell your home or pass away. Pre-payment penalties do apply if repayment is made early, similar to an early mortgage repayment of three months' interest or the interest rate differential.

Another option is a secured line of credit, which is available at most financial institutions for prime (currently 2.7 percent) plus one-half of 1 percent, or 3.2 percent. The big advantage of the secured line of credit over the reverse mortgage is the rate of interest charged. However, the necessity for income verification and the cost of regular loan repayments make a secured line of credit more difficult to obtain for seniors living on a fixed income.

In order to compete with a reverse mortgage, a few financial institutions have developed newer, innovative solutions. Outlined below is one such product, which offers a compelling alternative. The advantage of this particular HELOC is that no appraisal or legal fees apply under certain conditions, other than a $7 monthly service fee. As well, income verification and loan balance repayments have been made very accommodative. Speak to your financial advisor for more information.

TABLE 4.4
CHIP Reverse Mortgage versus Alternative HELOC Comparison

	CHIP Reverse Mortgage[1]	Alternative HELOC[2]
Eligibility	Over 55	Over 18
Appraisal Fee	$200–$400	None
Fees	Closing and administration $995	$7 per month over age 60
Interest Rate	Prime plus 2.20%	Prime plus 0.50%
Credit Limit	Up to 55% of appraisal value	50% of appraisal value up to 80%
Maximum Amount	Same as credit limit	Threshold is $1 million
Access to Funds	Regular payments or lump sum	ATM, debit, chequing, online
Repayment	Sale or death	At least one payment per year
Pre-payment Penalty	Applicable	None
Income Verification	None	Minimum requirement
Independent Legal Advice	$700–$1,000	Not required under 75

[1] Source for CHIP Reverse Mortgage information: www.chip.ca
[2] This particular HELOC is not typical of most and is only available through one financial institution that I am aware of.

* * *

I have written a great deal about the specifics of an individual's ability to retire comfortably and provided ideas on how to accomplish that successfully. However, this book is about creating wealth by properly investing in the stock market — in addition to investing in real estate and starting your own business, it still remains the best way to do so. The next chapter is where the rubber hits the road. I start by discussing when and why markets become overvalued and undervalued, and what indicators to pay attention to in order to draw your own conclusions. Of course, I also provide you with my own opinion based on over thirty years of being a student of the market. So now the journey begins. This is where things really get exciting!

5

ECONOMIC INDICATORS

As an investment strategy, buy-and-hold has not worked for at least two decades, so continuing with this strategy is not a good idea. It's commonly said that the definition of insanity is doing the same thing over and over and expecting different results.

If you want to be a successful investor, be mindful when listening to the so-called experts. Many of them have an agenda, and it won't always align with yours. You need to adopt other strategies. In the following pages, I will reveal many industry secrets that will help you to figure out what strategy works best for you. These secrets are ones that the financial industry doesn't want you to know.

Although there are problems in the market, it is not all bad news. There is opportunity! The economic indicators I describe in this chapter will provide you with a tremendous advantage. Don't misunderstand what I'm saying: this is not a "get rich quick" book. You will still need to appreciate and respect the natural order of things. The secrets I'm about to share will challenge you to use restraint, summon extreme discipline, and test your emotional fortitude. This book will push you to reach your full potential. In return, you will greatly increase your odds of achieving a level of wealth you've only imagined. You'll be able to retire on your terms!

Listed here are the compounded growth rates for both the ten- and twenty-year periods of the S&P TSX, S&P 500, and Dow Jones Industrial Average.

TABLE 5.1

The Lost Decades

January 1, 2006–January 1, 2016 (10 Years)

S&P TSX	1.15%
S&P 500	4.70%
DJIA	4.75%

January 1, 1996–January 1, 2016 (20 Years)

S&P TSX	2.45%
S&P 500	4.09%
DJIA	4.10%

As I have mentioned, the last decade has been named "the Lost Decade" due to poor investment returns. In other words, investing in the Canadian stock market for ten years starting in January 2006 returned 1.15 percent compounded annually. Investing in the U.S. stock market for the same period returned 4.7 percent compounded annually — relatively better, but still not close to historical averages. Coincidentally, that period began approximately one year before the market top in 2007. Investors are in the same position today. There is a good reason it is called the Lost Decade. Fortunately, the next decade doesn't have to be another disappointment. An excellent opportunity is waiting just around the corner.

THE BUFFETT INDICATOR

What do you see when you look at Figure 5.1? The chart shows the Wilshire 5000 Full Cap Price Index, which is a very broad-based U.S. index of 5,000 companies — a measure of the stock market's capitalization — crisscrossing the U.S. gross domestic product (GDP) with economic cycles, all while the economy continues growing at a constant rate over time. However, looking at this information more closely suggests a much more interesting picture.

There definitely seems to be a relationship between the stock market capitalization exceeding the GDP and the probability of a market correction. For example, in the years 1998, 2000, 2007, and 2013, the market capitalization of the Wilshire 5000 overtook GDP. These incidents forecast the Russian debt crisis in 1998, the Y2K tech bubble bursting in 2000, the housing crisis in 2008, and what may come next.

Conversely, when the market capitalization fell considerably below the GDP, such as in 1995, 2002, and again in 2009, the odds of a strong market recovery were quite good. These periods preceded the technology hysteria of the late nineties, the mid-2000 real estate–backed market bubble, and the current central bank–induced asset bubble.

FIGURE 5.1

Wilshire 5000 Full Cap Price Index as a Ratio of U.S. GDP

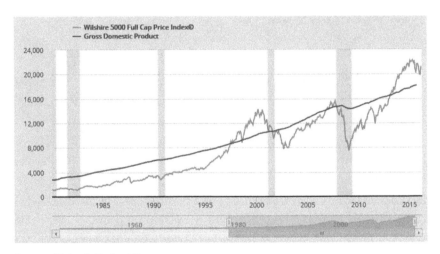

Source: St. Louis Federal Reserve

Figure 5.2 shows the ratio of the Wilshire 5000 Full Cap Price Index to the GDP. This ratio is otherwise known as "the Buffett Indicator." It earned its moniker from Warren Buffett himself, who said it is "probably the best single measure of where valuations stand at any given moment." Observe that on the dates mentioned earlier, when market premiums or extremes occurred, the indicator registered a ratio of more than 1:1.3 in 2000 and more than 1:1 in 2007, and, most recently, it exceeded a ratio of 1:1.2 in 2015.

FIGURE 5.2

The Buffett Indicator

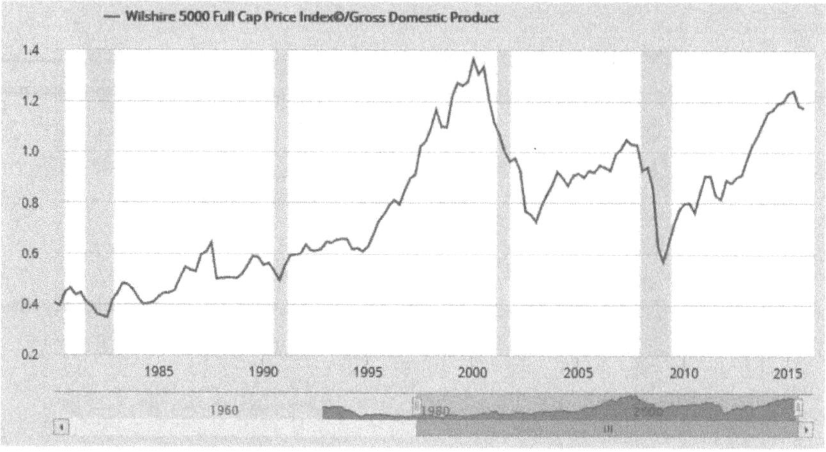

Source: St. Louis Federal Reserve

The reverse is also true: buying at a discounted ratio of just above 0.6 times in 1995, just above 0.7 times in 2002, and just below 0.6 times in 2009 resulted in substantial market gains.

All of this helps explain the "Lost Decade" returns many investors have experienced throughout the last twenty years. Those paying the highest premium on GDP, such as those who bought in 2000 and 2007, experienced abysmal ten-year returns. Investors buying GDP at a discount, such as in 1995, 2002, and 2009, made large gains.

Looking at where the ratio is currently, just below 1:1.2, it is clear that considerable caution is warranted. Purchasing equities at this overpriced level could lead you to become an investor of another lost decade. Don't make that mistake. Be patient. You will be well rewarded when the opportunity inevitably presents itself in the not-too-distant future.

Just as there are two sides to every coin, there are two arguments to every valuation model. Therefore, in this chapter I have provided many different ways to measure the market and the economy so that you can make an informed decision. I know my bias leans toward a pessimistic market outlook. It's not because I'm a naysayer; it's because I believe the market is due for a healthy correction. Experience tells me so. I've seen this type of behaviour before, both from the market and from industry experts. When the market rolls over and investors start to panic, the excuse is always the same: "How could I have possibly known that was going to happen?" Just remember: that's your money circling the market drain and not theirs. If you agree with me that the bulk of the gains are behind us, like even some extremely bullish analysts are suggesting, then why not get out while you still can? Take some profits. What are you waiting for? If not now, when?

*　*　*

Almost all economists and analysts interviewed in the media today are hanging off every data point that gets released, a habit referred to as "data dependency." So are the central banks. But they're all missing one very important point that makes all their arguments erroneous. Since 1987, almost all market corrections have not been the result of a weakening economy or fundamentals, but the product of exogenous shocks. These shocks were first called "black swans" by Nassim Taleb, a hedge fund manager and author of the book *The Black Swan*.

In 1987, the market experienced Black Monday. Did an economic data point cause the market to drop 20 percent in one day? In 1998, Long Term Capital Management collapsed under the weight of too much leverage and had to be rescued by U.S. Federal Reserve chair Alan Greenspan. In 2000, the economy was doing quite well, from what I recall. It was investor psychology that played a major role in both the mania and devastation, not the economy. Finally, in 2007, perpetuated greed caused the collapse of real estate prices, not a weak economic backdrop.

What I'm talking about is systemic risk. What's the difference between systemic risk and normal or "unsystemic" risk? Normal risk is specific to an individual company or country, caused by the decisions made by the leadership of that particular company or country. Systemic risk has the potential to spread, like cancer, from the grievous errors corporations or governments make to other corporations or countries, due to their magnitude, with or without intent. Systemic risk is not something that can be meaningfully understood until after the fact. However, we can postulate on what the potential threats may be. A systemic risk can exert overwhelming influence on the complicated web of global finance. Manifestations of systemic risk that can undermine entire economies include government monetary policy that leads to misallocation of capital, abandonment of the law by corporations, debt-enhanced financial engineering, currency manipulation, terrorism, and, of course, investor stampedes caused by some extreme action or event or some mass psychological change.

All of this raises the question: How big of a threat does systemic risk pose to the market today? According to a poll recently conducted by the CFA (Chartered Financial Analyst) Institute's Enterprising Investor blog, 85 percent of respondents indicated that a medium to high risk of an imminent crisis existed as a result of systemic risk.

MONETARY POLICY AND THE LAW OF UNINTENDED CONSEQUENCES

Many pundits today would argue that the central banks' artificially low interest rate policies have created massive asset bubbles and, in doing so, have created tremendous systemic risk. John Maynard Keynes so fittingly said, "Markets can remain irrational longer than you and I can remain solvent." His statement underlines the fact that betting against a reversal in a market trend is a risky proposition and can lead to substantial loss.

Keynes's observation is of great help for guiding individual investors when confronting market downturns. However, Keynes is much better known for his observations regarding the appropriate action for a state to take when confronted with a depressed economy. According to Keynesian economics, state intervention is warranted to moderate the "boom and bust" cycles of economic activity. Further, Keynes advocated the use of fiscal and monetary policies to mitigate the adverse effects of economic recessions or even depressions.

Since the Second World War, the central banks of most Western countries have followed Keynes's recommendations on how best to regulate their economies. In the United States, the propensity of the U.S. Federal Reserve to use its power to stimulate the economy has given rise to the expression "Don't fight the Fed." Its success in stimulating the economy is open to argument, but its stimulation measures have certainly had an impact on the stock market.

A central bank's primary purpose is to control a country's monetary policy, and it usually has several mandates, including, but not limited to, issuing the country's national currency, maintaining the value of the currency, ensuring financial system stability, controlling credit supply, and serving as a lender of last resort. Over the last thirty years, central banks, both in North America and abroad, have used monetary policy to save the global stock markets from collapse. The safe continuance of central banks has enabled market participants to continue to behave poorly, resulting in their complete dependency.

The United States is Canada's largest trading partner, and whatever happens south of the border directly affects Canada. Our Bank of Canada governors since 1994 — Gordon Thiessen, David Dodge, Mark Carney, and, currently, Stephen Poloz — have simply mirrored U.S. stimulus measures. Considering Canada was never at the epicentre of the financial crisis in 2008 due to tighter banking controls, we did not experience similar extremes, such as the collapse of any of our financial institutions. Unfortunately, what we have inherited because of the same monetary policies is inflated asset prices.

In 2013, Janet Yellen became the first female Federal Reserve chair. The United States has had seven years of zero interest rate policy (ZIRP), and it can be argued that it has been one of the weakest recoveries in history. There has been little to no GDP growth, inflation, job creation, or investment in business innovation. What have been created, though, are inflated asset bubbles everywhere, particularly in the equity and real estate markets. What have real estate prices risen to in Toronto and Vancouver? A teardown in my neighbourhood in Toronto is fetching $875,000. The average price for a home in Vancouver is $1.4 million. At these prices, many first-time home buyers simply do not have the means to purchase any home at all. Unfortunately, those who have overextended themselves will soon face some very difficult decisions.

Mario Draghi of the European Central Bank and Haruhiko Kuroda of the Bank of Japan have also both been notably accommodative; in other words, they have used extreme measures of monetary stimulus to create growth and inflation. Despite these accommodative measures, the desired effects have not been achieved. In fact, the complete opposite has occurred. Historically, low interest rates would have devalued currencies, causing goods to become cheaper and stimulating economic growth. Bond purchases would have driven down yields and encouraged borrowing. Instead, what has transpired is a negative-feedback loop. The more stimulus that Europe and Japan have unveiled, the more their currencies have strengthened, their economic conditions have deteriorated, and loan growth to the private sector has decreased — and the response to all of this has been further stimulus.

Japan and Europe, as well as periphery European Union countries, have now resorted to NIRP (negative interest rate policy), ZIRP's cousin. What this has caused is a doubled effort of cash hoarding. This is a slippery slope, and if improvements are not seen shortly, deflation could begin to accelerate. Essentially, the consequences of deflation are falling prices, reduced spending, and inventory build-up. This results in job losses, higher unemployment, and an economic freeze.

What is most worrisome about this scenario is that central banks have already exhausted a lot of their ammunition. This is what I believe is causing considerable fear within the closed-door meetings of central bankers.

The People's Bank of China (PBOC) has had its own issues to deal with of late. The Shanghai Stock Exchange plummeted 50 percent during 2015. Some speculators, experiencing their first bear market, had to be rescued. China's GDP growth has been falling for six years, declining from an annual rate of increase of 12 percent to one of 6.7 percent, and the yuan has been under attack from both U.S. dollar depreciation and capital outflows. In response, the PBOC has experimented with circuit breakers (backstopping market declines by shutting down the stock exchange temporarily), stop-gap measures, bank reserve reductions, currency manipulation, and state-owned enterprise bail-outs. As a result of the severe economic slowdown, reform of the economy, transitioning it from one with a manufacturing base to a consumer-based one, has been pushed aside, while economic stimulus in the form of additional debt creation is diverted to support capital investments and exports.

To understand the relationship between the PBOC and the United States, we do not have to look any further than the foreign exchange market. The exchange rate between the U.S. dollar and the Chinese yuan has been fixed for several years. To maintain this peg, the PBOC has had to constantly intervene. It is not known what the real exchange rate would be between the yuan and the dollar without intervention. What *is* known is that the U.S. dollar would depreciate considerably. In order to prevent this from happening, the PBOC has had to keep buying U.S. dollars. This has created a wonderfully symbiotic relationship, considering the United States has continually needed to borrow money to fund its ongoing deficits. The U.S. trade deficit imbalance with China might ordinarily have pushed up the value of the yuan, but China has prevented this from happening by buying hundreds of billions in U.S. dollar–denominated treasuries.

So, the question on everyone's mind is, "Why does China fix its exchange rate?" The standard answer is that China sees a fixed exchange rate as a way of achieving a low inflation rate. By fixing the yuan against the U.S. dollar, China's inflation rate is anchored to the U.S. inflation rate. The truth is, China fixes the yuan in order to keep its export prices low. If, on the other hand, China were to start aggressively selling U.S. treasuries, the price would drop, causing yields to rise, resulting in considerable losses. If America's plan is to get their economy on better footing, they may soon have to take a tougher stance with China.

What this means for you is that, if it does occur, it will provide an opportunity to increase your net worth dramatically in a relatively short period of time. It's not a question of "if" at this point; it's a question of "what" and "when."

Of course, monetary policy has a significant impact on the velocity with which money flows into and out of a country, all of which can, in turn, have a considerable effect on a nation's economic stability. Monetary policy, or, more specifically, interest rate policy, can dramatically affect the flow of money, all things being equal. For example, increasing interest rates attract money and vice versa. Another way to measure this is by the balance of payments. A country's balance of payments records its importing, exporting, borrowing, and lending activities. The current account records importing and exporting activities and income paid abroad. The capital account records the difference between a nation's foreign investment and the investment it receives from abroad. A country that is borrowing more from the rest of the world than lending to it is called a net borrower. Currently, both the United States and Canada are net borrowers. Countries that are net lenders to the world include China, Japan, and Saudi Arabia.

So should we be concerned that Canada and the United States are debtors? The answer to the question depends on what the net borrower is doing with the money. If borrowing leads to economic growth and earns a return that covers the interest, it is not a problem. However, if the borrowed money is used to finance consumption, make entitlement payments, and pay the interest and principal on existing loans, consumption will eventually have to be reduced. The longer this continues, the greater the reduction in consumption. The next question is much more difficult to answer: When will we reach the tipping point?

If you are interested in learning more, an excellent online source for obtaining timely and historical economic data is www.tradingeconomics.com.

UNEMPLOYMENT RATE

The unemployment rate is defined as the number of unemployed people, expressed as a percentage of the total of both all the people who have jobs and those who are looking for them. Critics argue that the unemployment rate is unreliable and easily manipulated on two accounts. First, it excludes people who have given up looking for work. Second, it doesn't tell us about the number of part-time workers who want full-time jobs. The popular label for this new type of labour market — one that increasingly relies on part-time workers to fill companies' labour needs — is the "gig economy." The standard format of its employer–employee relationship contrasts with the norm of another era: a full-time job, with benefits, that folks used to keep for years.

The highest level ever recorded for the unemployment rate occurred during the Great Depression of the 1930s, when it climbed to 25 percent in the United States. Although rates have fallen considerably since then, even at the best of times — when so-called "full employment" is realized — the unemployment rate still never falls to zero. This may seem counter-intuitive. The reason for this seeming contradiction is that full employment is defined as a period when no cyclical unemployment is perceptible. Cyclical unemployment is unemployment that is caused by the extremes of a recession or during an extended expansion.

The cycle in Canadian unemployment is highly correlated to that of the United States. Since the Second World War, the average unemployment rate has been about 5.8 percent in the United States — approximately 2 percent lower than the Canadian unemployment rate, which has averaged about 7.7 percent.

FIGURE 5.3
Unemployment Rate: Canada

Source: Tradingeconomics.com; Statistics Canada

FIGURE 5.4
Unemployment Rate: United States

Source: Tradingeconomics.com; U.S. Bureau of Labor Statistics

Why is the unemployment rate so important? As it turns out, hitting a trough in the unemployment rate has been a very good indicator of the next recession. Many economic indicators have flashed false warning signals due to the distortions in the market and continual stimulus measures. They include peak auto sales, housing starts, GDP, interest rates, and inflation. However, the one constant in the economy is the speed at which the labour market heals itself.

The unemployment rate in the United States has fallen at an average pace of 0.7 percent, according to David Kelly, chief global strategist at J.P. Morgan Funds, during the last seven expansions since 1960. More recently, the unemployment rate has been falling at a steady pace of 0.8 percent per year for more than six years and has now declined to 5 percent. If this trend were to continue, it would put the unemployment rate at 4.2 percent by the end of 2016, just below the average trough unemployment rate of 4.5 percent.

We have not yet had any wage gains, but if we were to see signs of wage inflation, it is likely that the Federal Reserve would start to increase interest rates in order to attempt to engineer a "soft landing." Once rates started to move higher, we could expect to find ourselves in a recession within a year. Remember that the Fed is generally too slow to tighten, and the market would be ahead of the curve by a few months. This would suggest significant recession risk in 2017.

On another related matter, for the week ended April 16, 2016, the number of Americans filing for unemployment insurance, otherwise known as "initial jobless claims," was 247,000 — the lowest reading since 1973. This is an important number because it measures new and emerging unemployment, as opposed to continuing claims from those of the unemployed who have yet to find work. The low number of initial jobless claims is further evidence of a strong employment picture and the likelihood that full employment will soon be reached, if it has not already.

FIGURE 5.5
U.S. Initial Jobless Claims

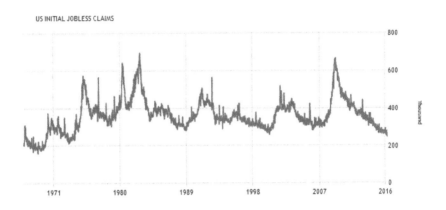

Source: Tradingeconomics.com; U.S. Department of Labor

Some also point out that this low level of claims comes against a much larger working-age population than existed forty-three years ago. Thus, the implication is that the labour market is even stronger than the claims data suggest.

TRANSPORTATION SLOWDOWN

The Baltic Dry Index (BDI) is a topic that comes up from time to time on television and in the occasional newspaper article. So what is the BDI anyway? Well, it is many things, actually. The textbook definition of the BDI is that it is a measure of the cost of shipping raw materials, such as metals, grains, and fossil fuels, by dry bulk carriers. What it tells us is much more.

Based on the principle of supply and demand, when the economy is booming, lots of goods are being shipped, and the cost of shipping those goods becomes greater. Conversely, when the economy is slow or in a recession, very few goods are being transported, and shipping costs fall. Therefore, the cost of shipping goods should be a good indication of the strength or weakness of the economy.

The BDI is not only a measure of current economic activity; it is also a useful predictor of future economic activity — freighters are not booked unless people have cargo to move — and so it is termed a leading economic indicator.

FIGURE 5.6
Baltic Dry Index

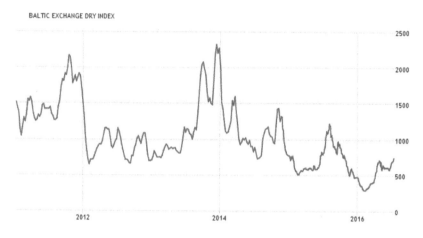

BALTIC EXCHANGE DRY INDEX

Source: Tradingeconomics.com; Baltic Exchange

During the commodity boom in May 2008, the BDI reached an all-time high of 11,793. Just over half a year later, in December 2008, the index had dropped by 94 percent, to 663 points. It's now eight years later and the index is currently sitting at 671, which is cause for concern, considering these low rates are close to the operating costs of vessels. How could this happen, and what are the implications?

During the boom times of the commodity cycle that drove oil up to $147 per barrel and gold to $1,895, many shipping operators ordered additional vessels, believing the good times would continue. By the time the new vessels were being delivered a few years later, commodity prices had already collapsed. Some pundits argue that the low current shipping rates are not necessarily a result of low commodity prices as much as an oversupply of ships. This would suggest that the global economy is not as weak as some believe.

Another index, the HARPEX, is a measure of container freight rates. The demand for container ships by producers who need their goods shipped to market is another indicator of the health of the global economy. Containers typically carry a wide variety of finished goods from a multitude of sellers. These are finished goods headed for the retail market, at the other end of the supply chain. It shouldn't come as a surprise that the HARPEX is not far from its lows either, at 360, down over 40 percent from one year ago.

If, however, commodity prices are not the cause of the low BDI and HARPEX shipping rates, but, rather, a glut of vessels, then shouldn't commodity prices be stable? Shouldn't rail freight volumes be level? Shouldn't truck sales be robust as carriers replace aging fleets? Yet none of these are true.

An index called the Thomson Reuters Core Commodity CRB Index, a well-known measure of global commodity prices, has been tracking a basket of commodities for nearly half a century. It comprises nineteen components of varied weightings, the heaviest being agriculture at 41 percent, followed by energy at 39 percent, industrial metals at 13 percent, and precious metals at 7 percent.

TABLE 5.2

Components of Thomson Reuters Core Commodity CRB Index

19 Components	Weighting (%)
Crude Oil	23
Corn	6
Soybeans	6
Aluminum	6
⌐ Copper	6
Live Cattle	6
Gold	6
Natural Gas	6
RBOB Gasoline	5
Sugar	5
Cotton	5
Coffee	5
Cocoa	5
Heating Oil	5

19 Components	Weighting (%)
Wheat	1
Nickel	1
Orange Juice	1
Silver	1
Lean Hogs	1
Totals	
Agriculture	41
Energy	39
Industrial Metals	13
Precious Metals	7

The CRB Index is currently trading at 180. This is just off the lows of 155 reached in February 2016 and 50 percent lower than the level reached in late 2011. The last time the index was at this level was in November 2002, fourteen years ago. The all-time high was recorded in July 2008, at 473. Since that time the index has fallen 62 percent.

FIGURE 5.7
Thomson Reuters Core Commodity CRB Index

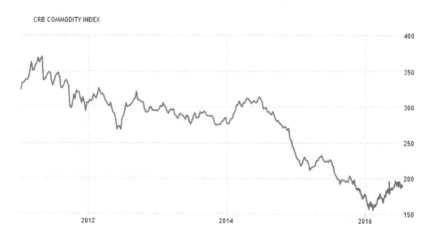

Source: Tradingeconomics.com; Thomson Reuters

The fall of the index may be an indication not only of slowing economic growth, but also of deflation. Despite the attempts of central banks to stimulate the world economy and produce inflation, their efforts have proven ineffective. In my opinion, time is running out before the next credit event occurs and markets are sent reeling, similar to in 2008.

Some unusual events are occurring in the railroad industry as well. Recently railcar orders have been dropping, as evidenced by data from two railcar makers, Trinity Industries Inc. and Greenbrier Companies. The pressure on orders has come from lower demand for coal, crude oil, and metals, and the strong U.S. dollar. In 2016, carload volumes declined — there was a drop of more than 5 percent during the summer in 2016 on a year-over-year basis. A similar decline has not occurred since 2009.

Many would argue that the slowdown in the fossil fuel boom would naturally lead to fewer goods being moved by rail. However, there are signs that the slowdown is spreading beyond bulk freight rail transport to more consumer-oriented, intermodal (container) carloads. For the second week of April 2016, intermodal carloads were off by 7.4 percent, as reported by the Association of American Railroads.

FIGURE 5.8
Rail Freight Carloads

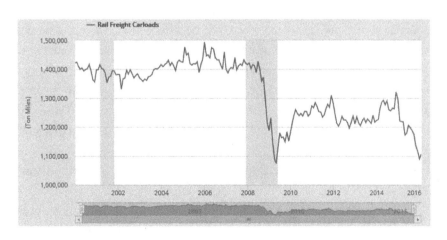

Source: St. Louis Federal Reserve; U.S. Bureau of Transportation Statistics

FIGURE 5.9
Rail Freight Intermodal Traffic

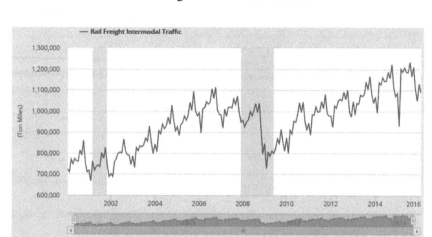

Source: St. Louis Federal Reserve; U.S. Bureau of Transportation Statistics

Canada has not escaped the pending slowdown. In the first quarter of 2016, Canadian railroads reported a decrease of 5.3 percent in rail traffic volume year over year, including containers and trailers. This is attributed largely to a drop in coal shipments, but it is indicative of a decline across all product lines.

Perhaps the clearest window on the state of things is that offered by the source itself — railcar traffic in China. Alas, rail freight volume is collapsing. It is no secret that the GDP numbers reported by China are suspect. Whatever the real number is, we know one thing for sure: the number is in decline. According to data from China Railway Corporation, rail freight volume fell 10.5 percent in 2015 and is on course to drop another 9.4 percent this year. That's almost 20 percent from 2014, which had already been a down year. What is evident is that China continues to prop up its economy with massive amounts of debt as it attempts to transition from a manufacturing economy to an economy based on consumption. Whether it is able to succeed is another matter.

Not only are rail freight levels declining around the world, but, according to the International Air Transport Association, released demand growth data for global air freight markets for March 2016 showed a 2 percent drop in volume, as measured in freight tonne kilometres, compared to the same period last year. The most significant fall in demand was reported by carriers in Asia-Pacific and North America. Combined, the two regions account for around 60 percent of global freight traffic and have reported declines of 5.2 percent and 1.8 percent, respectively. This information confirms, despite the rhetoric, that China's economy is slowing considerably and that that of the United States is dangerously close to stalling. Moreover, the export orders component of the global Purchasing Managers' Index, a closely watched business survey that has a long-standing relationship with growth in air freight volumes, remained in contractionary territory for the second consecutive month in March 2016.

One final topic that needs to be looked at is the struggling trucking industry. There are massive inventory builds of long-haul trucks on dealers' lots. Sales in March 2016 dropped 37 percent from a year earlier. Companies that placed large orders for trucks in late 2014, only to see customers move less freight than expected the following year, are reluctant to buy more vehicles now, say analysts. Although the Dow Transports index has seen a tremendous rally from the February 2016 lows, truck manufacturers like PACCAR Inc. (whose brands include Kenworth and Peterbilt) and Navistar see continued pressure on their share prices. On a similar note, online freight marketplace DAT Solutions reported last month that spot market rates for box trucks that travel all U.S. highways fell 18 percent between February 2015 and February 2016. An obvious conclusion is that, despite all the talk of an economic recovery — albeit a slow one — the facts simply do not confirm this. In fact, the economy is on precarious ground, and we could be in store for a recession sooner than we'd like.

STEEL PRODUCTION

World steel production is usually a good indicator of how the global economy is faring. At present, the supply of steel hitting the market is at an all-time high, and the demand is at a multi-year low. As a result, the price of steel is at levels not seen since the last recession — despite the fact that GDP and global equity markets continue to defy gravity.

The overcapacity in steel production can be attributed to a couple of factors. First, the fall in oil prices has eliminated the need for steel in rigs and pipelines. Second, even though demand growth in China is unlikely to recover to prior years' levels, when the country first embarked on a debt-fuelled infrastructure construction binge, production at Chinese steel mills has continued unabated. This raises a number of concerns for the future. With prices at these levels, steel producers from other developing countries, not to mention those from Western Europe and North America, are not able to compete. Unprofitable foundries will eventually have to be shut down, causing massive layoffs, all of which raises the possibility of trade wars, tariffs, subsidies, and government bail-outs, when what is really needed is structural change or a full-scale overhaul.

CAPACITY UTILIZATION

Let's suppose you are the owner of a company that manufactures Toronto Blue Jays baseball caps. In 2015 you had a great year as the Blue Jays became hopefuls for the American League Championship. You received sizable orders.

Even with the sizable orders, however, it was only necessary to keep your plant running at 85 percent capacity. If you had been making as many caps as possible each day — running at 100 percent capacity — you would have been able to make 1,000 caps per day. Instead, you were producing 850. As a result of the disappointing loss to Kansas City and the end of the season, orders slowed considerably. So you cut production and began running the plant at 75 percent of capacity, producing 750 units.

Unfortunately, this year, demand for baseball caps didn't seem as strong as it did last year at first. If they didn't have a good year, you were afraid that demand for Jays caps would drop further and more cost-cutting would be necessary to avoid losing money, which would not rule out employee layoffs. Miraculously, the Jays pulled through late in the season, and no production cuts or layoffs were necessary.

Capacity utilization is said to be an excellent gauge of the health of the economy, since it measures the output of existing factories. Measured as a percentage, if factories are cranking on all cylinders, so to say, utilization should be at 100 percent. As it drops lower, it means that factories are sitting idle or not producing as much as they could be. This can be interpreted as a measure of demand: if demand is sluggish, then factories will produce fewer goods.

Capacity utilization in Canada has averaged 82.48 percent for the last twenty-eight years. In the fourth quarter of 2015, capacity utilization decreased to 81.1 percent from 82 percent in the third quarter of 2015. It can be argued that the recent decline has come from one sector, energy. So the question remains: Will the other segments of Canada's economy keep GDP growth positive, or will the energy slump be responsible for a more protracted slowdown?

FIGURE 5.10
Capacity Utilization: Canada

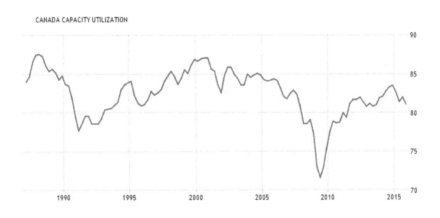

CANADA CAPACITY UTILIZATION

Source: Tradingeconomics.com; Statistics Canada

In the United States we can observe a similar theme. Capacity utilization there averaged 80.44 percent for the last forty-six years. In the first quarter of 2016, it decreased to 74.8 percent in March from 75.4 percent in February.

FIGURE 5.11
Capacity Utilization: United States

Source: Tradingeconomics.com; Federal Reserve

It should be highlighted that, throughout the years that capacity utilization data has been available, a fall in magnitude equal to current readings has always coincided with a recession.

THE HOUSING BUBBLE

Economists consider housing prices another important sign of the health of an economy. Inflated housing prices pose a risk to stable economic growth. In Canada, housing prices have been rising at an accelerated rate for a considerable period now. As a result, many have concluded that there is a housing bubble in this country, particularly in Vancouver and Toronto.

Notice that I didn't title this section "Is Real Estate Overvalued?" or "How Much Higher Can Real Estate Prices Get?" Let me be perfectly clear. The price of real estate in Canada is overvalued. Period! The only question is, "When will it end?" I suspect not until we experience the next credit event, recession, financial collapse, market correction, or whatever you want to call it. Fill in the blank.

For the time being, however, there is no question that the real estate market in Canada is overvalued. There has certainly been lots of media discussion of the problem of late. Included in that has been some interesting claims. For example, an odd measure that the media have been headlining for a while now to determine real estate overvaluation is the household debt-to-gross-income ratio, which is at 167 percent. This is the equivalent of having $500,000 in total debt outstanding and an annual household income of $300,000. According to Statscan, the average for the last twenty-five years has been about 123 percent, which would make the current reading 36 percent overvalued. According to the *Economist*, compared with rents, the household interest paid to disposable income is overvalued by 89 percent. The reason I believe these measures to be odd is that they are not at all used in practice to determine a homebuyer's ability to fund a mortgage.

The measures to determine affordability of real estate for homebuyers by Canadian lenders are the total debt service ratio (TDSR) and the gross debt service ratio (GDSR); they are, practically speaking, much better affordability indicators. These calculations are arrived at by dividing debt payments by gross monthly income. The TDSR includes all existing monthly debt payments, such as payments for auto, lines of credit, credit cards, loans, and any other monthly obligations, as well as housing-related payments. If the ratio is less than 40 percent, you are considered a good credit risk. The GDSR is the percentage of income required to cover payments associated with housing costs. These costs include mortgages, property taxes, utilities, fees, and any other housing-related monthly obligations. This ratio should be less than 32 percent of gross monthly income.

Unfortunately, the law of unintended consequences has had a significant effect on the real estate market in the last few years. What has occurred is that low interest rates, designed to make home ownership more affordable, have driven housing prices to nosebleed levels. Let me explain with an example. When rates were at 5 percent, a typical house was priced at a level so that, along with a decent down payment, a mortgage of $300,000 was sufficient. With this mortgage, a monthly payment ran you about $1,750. However, the same property today, with the same down payment, is priced so that a $500,000 mortgage is required. You may be able to get a mortgage at half the interest cost, or 2.5 percent, but the monthly mortgage payment is about $2,200, a 28 percent increase. I'm not even going to mention what will happen if interest rates begin to rise.

Another major contributor to today's financial asset bubbles, which include real estate, is the flow of capital into a market, which is often the product of the flight of capital from other markets. This movement of capital is, of course, a symptom of political systems that are beginning to self-destruct. If a large amount of your net worth was in a country in which the government could expropriate it at any moment, where currency devaluation could make it worth considerably less, or where it could be used to save a financial system from failing — commonly referred to as a "bail-in" — what would you do? That's what I thought: you'd move your money out of the country.

Recently, Canada has seen a considerable inflow of money from wealthy citizens of countries that are considered less secure. One country in particular stands out. There's no need to name the elephant in the room. Its flag, like that of many other unstable countries, is red.

The good news with all of this is that, for those who are patient, real estate, just like the stock market, will present a great buying opportunity when the present housing bubble does explode. The decision to buy a home should, however (in most cases, at least), depend on your reason. If the purpose of buying a house is so that you can own a principal residence, then you must buy a home. A principal residence is the only investment that can be sold tax-free, uses leverage, and can house you and your family. If you are buying the property for investment purposes, then you'll be disappointed. The stock market will outperform real estate by many multiples, as it always has.

A more unorthodox indication that the real estate market is overvalued is the number of registered real estate agents in the Greater Toronto Area. When every Tom, Dick, and Susie believes he or she can get into a hot industry and make tons of money, that is as good a sign as any that the market is overvalued.

The securities industry experienced a similar trend in the late 1990s. I remember that a young broker I worked with asked me to come down to the parking lot to see his new wheels. At that time, the markets were on fire, and some hot shots were pulling in $20,000 to $30,000 a month. He was driving a brand new Mercedes CLK. I'm not a huge car guy, but it seemed pretty nice to me. Do I need to tell you what happened next? In three months the car was gone; in six months, so was he. This was about the same time every stay-at-home mom and cabbie was day trading his or her online account into hundreds of thousands. Their stories didn't end well either. The moral of the story is that there is no easy money to be made.

Here are some statistics for those with a similar mindset to ponder. There are now 42,000 licensed real estate agents in the GTA, a record high. That compares to 20,000 a decade ago. Even with the increase in the price of houses, the fact that there are so many more agents competing for each deal means that making money selling real estate is much more difficult these days. If you were to sell a $1 million house, with a 5 percent commission, that would put $50,000 gross into your pocket. That sounds pretty good. More realistically, however, the commission on that deal would be split with another agent and you would earn 2.5 percent.

Now the cold hard truth: 57 percent of all agents sell fewer than three homes per year, and one-third of agents don't sell anything at all.

Right before the 2007 housing collapse, every channel on television seemed to have a show titled *Flip This* or *Sell That*. Not long after, many seemed to disappear. Lately I've noticed that many are back again. Look, I think home ownership is a wonderful privilege and that everyone should aspire to become a homeowner. However, just like those working in the securities industry, a real estate agent or television personality is never going to tell you that the market is overheated. Especially when their livelihood depends on telling you what great a time it is to buy. They, too, are paid to be bullish.

Speculating on real estate is a risky, though potentially lucrative, form of investment. Doing the same with equities offers the same benefits and risks — in an even purer play.

THE CANADIAN DOLLAR EXCHANGE RATE

Thanks to an oil boom, the Canadian dollar appreciated from US$0.78 to US$1.05, or 33 percent, between February 1, 2009, and July 1, 2011. If you were holding U.S. stocks during that time period, you didn't notice the drag on your return due to the astonishing move from the March 2009 lows. However, that does not negate the fact that you gave up 33 percent of your return to the appreciation of the Canadian dollar. Another reason many overlooked this move in the value of the Canadian dollar is that it just as quickly reversed course — as a result of an oil bust this time — and depreciated from US$1.05 back down to US$0.71 between July 1, 2011, and January 1, 2016. If you were holding U.S. assets during this period, you certainly noticed, as both performance and currency played in your favour.

FIGURE 5.12

Value of Canadian Dollar versus Crude Oil Prices

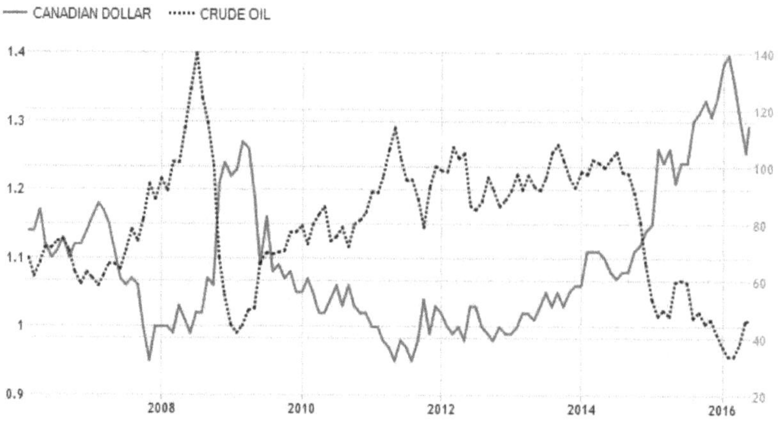

Source: Tradingeconomics.com

Even if you did not invest in U.S. equities in 2011, simply purchasing U.S. dollars would have earned you a nice return of 47 percent.

Historically, the Canadian dollar reached an all-time low of US$0.62 in January 2002 and a record high of US$1.08 in November 2007. Generally, when the Canadian dollar has appreciated to par or above the U.S. dollar, it has been a slam dunk to buy U.S. dollars. Currency direction is extremely difficult to predict. However, when the Canadian dollar is at extremes, either at par or better or at US$0.70 or less, currency valuations should be a serious consideration when making investment decisions. If you are considering buying U.S. assets when the Canadian dollar is low, hedging should be considered, as any appreciation in the Canadian dollar may reduce or eliminate any U.S. dollar profits. There are many investment products available in the marketplace today that give you both hedged and non-hedged options for very little additional expense.

The same situation is true for interest rates. Predicting interest rate direction is also next to impossible. Case in point: we have never seen negative interest rates at any other time in history. If we use Japan as an example of what may happen to interest rates in Canada and in the United

States, we should not discount a negative interest rate policy. Both Janet Yellen and Stephen Poloz have commented that it should not be ruled out. We have a very serious problem with excessive amounts of debt in the world today. Central banks will never do what is required because of the lack of political will. Instead, they continue to feed the asset bubbles. This cycle may not end until the only available alternatives are to default, reflate, or re-structure. Default, in my opinion, is pretty much out of the question, and restructuring would be political suicide. Therefore, the easiest and most politically acceptable alternative is an attempt to reflate.

If you trust central banks to do "whatever it takes" to keep markets from destabilizing, or if confidence is completely lost, some extremely large outliers exist. As a consequence, we could potentially experience a dramatic rise in interest rates, which would generate inflation. This is why a lot of gold bugs are currently pounding the table and, for that matter, gold is showing signs of life. However, I think there is a better hedge to this potential threat than gold, and that is bonds. More specifically, shorting bonds. Recall that bond prices and interest rates are inversely related. Therefore, if interest rates go up, bond prices must fall. Further, bonds with the greatest price sensitivity to interest rates are ones with the longest maturities and lowest coupons or, for that matter, zero coupon or strip bonds — in other words, bonds that pay no interest.

There is a remote possibility that inflation could be the next catalyst for a crisis. If so, then real return bonds, or TIPS (treasury inflation protected securities) in the United States, are your investment choice. The values of these bonds are tied to the consumer price index. Although inflation and interest rates are inextricably tied together, you do not necessarily have to have both present at the same time. It is quite possible to have rising interest rates without inflation, as demonstrated by the recent actions of the Federal Reserve, or rising inflation without interest rates following closely, although that is rare. Recently, James Bullard himself, president of the Federal Reserve Bank of St. Louis, said that "the best measure of inflation expectations" (referring to TIPS) shows little sign of inflation hitting even the Fed's 2 percent target. Five-year TIPS are pricing in inflation of just 1.5 percent, while thirty-year TIPS are pricing in 1.8 percent inflation. However, that would change very quickly if confidence in the U.S. Federal Reserve began to falter.

Why would I choose bonds over gold? In a nutshell, leverage. You may be able to buy physical gold proxies or gold stocks on margin, but doing so won't get you anything that comes close to the face value of bonds that can be controlled with the same dollar amount. Trading gold bullion in a commodity brokerage account does offer comparable leverage, but shorting bonds can be done much more easily in a margin account. For example, with $5,000 of margin you can control a face value of $100,000 in GOC (Government of Canada) bonds. The potential is huge, but so is the risk!

There are some very smart hedge fund managers forecasting a bond bear market. I suspect that they are doing so for the same reasons gold bugs are predicting that the price of gold is going to $5,000. We are in unprecedented times. At no other time in recorded history has there been a situation in which interest rates have been negative. Moreover, there are no economic models or blueprints directing decision makers on what course of action they should take or what levers they should pull. As a result, we have central bankers around the world experimenting with policy tools, hoping that their actions will have efficacy. Unfortunately, their efforts have not created sustainable change and they're running out of dry powder. They are also becoming more data dependent. This leads to the question: Are they losing control?

The U.S. dollar has held the status of the world reserve currency since the Bretton Woods Agreement was signed after the Second World War. Despite predictions of the U.S. dollar's demise, the doom-and-gloom situation predicted never seems to come to pass. Instead, the U.S. dollar has strengthened significantly since 2014, doing so in the wake of economic headwinds in Greece, China, and other places around the globe. One bright spot is that any concerns about the loss of currency reserve status for the U.S. dollar can be put on hold for the foreseeable future. If this ever were to happen, who knows what events would be taking place globally?

* * *

Despite the fact that most economists and industry permabulls have been reporting on a regular basis for the past seven years that this is a strengthening, healthy economy, I have attempted to offer solid economic evidence that what lies beneath is less than sanguine. Let me remind you once again that I find it highly unlikely that the next downturn will be due to weakening economic conditions. Unfortunately, it is my opinion that central banks have created a recurring cycle of boom and bust from a continual manipulation of free markets and true price discovery.

Another possible reason why industry experts can lose sight of changing economic conditions can be found in behavioural finance and, more specifically, a condition known as anchoring. Anchoring is the study of how emotions and other extraneous factors, rather than rational theories and analysis, influence economic choices. For example, investors tend to hold investments that have lost value because they have anchored their fair value estimate to the original price rather than to the fundamentals or changing market conditions.

These are just two of the many possible explanations that will inevitably lead to the opportunity for those investors who are prepared to create tremendous wealth for themselves and their families. *How to Profit from the Next Bull Market* is the blueprint for that plan.

6

GETTING TECHNICAL

Technical analysis is not intended to be a major component of this book. There have been many books written on the subject already, and there is much controversy surrounding its predictive power. However, technical analysis, in conjunction with other tools such as fundamental analysis, which I tackle in the next chapter, has proven to be a valuable resource for many market professionals. If my hypothesis is correct, the strategy of purchasing high-quality equities at the beginning of a bull market means you shouldn't need to rely on technical analysis. However, understanding the trajectory of a stock in a market cycle may reduce the risk of investors making emotional decisions that turn out to be costly.

PATTERNS, WAVES, AND CYCLES

First, let's explore a few constants to warm up. We know that pi (or π), which represents the ratio of the circumference of a circle to its diameter, is equal to 3.14159. How do we know this for sure? Well, the Greek mathematician Archimedes was able to prove it with considerable accuracy two thousand years ago.

Now, with the number derived from his proof, we can do some extremely powerful calculations with a circle. For example, using π and radius (r), here are the formulas for a circle's circumference (C) and area (A):

$$C = 2\pi r \qquad\qquad A = \pi r^2$$

Another magical number, discovered by Leonhard Euler (pronounced "oiler"), is Euler's number, the natural logarithm (ln) e:

$$e = 2.71828$$

You may have seen this symbol before and not realized its usefulness. For my purposes, I'm going to be highlighting its application in compounding interest.

Referring back to the chapter on math, you'll recall that FV = $PV(1 + i)^n$. As helpful as this calculation is, it also has limitations. What if we need to calculate interest that compounded, or more likely accrued, on a semi-annual, quarterly, monthly, or even continuous basis?

Luckily, we can simply manipulate the formula to include periods of interest and time. For instance:

$$FV = PV\left(1 + \frac{1}{n}\right)^n$$

Now look what happens...

$$1\left(1 + \frac{1}{1000}\right)^{1000} = (1.001)^{1000} = 2.71692$$

So, if you want to know how much you would owe if a banker says to you that the interest rate on $1,000 borrowed at 5 percent for two years is compounded continuously, don't fret. Just use Euler's number:

$$FV = PV \times e^{rt} = \$1{,}000 \times e^{0.05*2}$$

You would owe $1,105.17, borrowing $1,000 for two years with an interest rate of 5 percent compounded continuously.

Another application for Euler's number is calculating how long it would take to compound a specific dollar amount. How long does it take to double your money earning 9 percent interest, for example? Using the Rule of 72, we know the answer is approximately eight years.

$$\frac{\ln 2}{\ln 1.09} = 8.043 \text{ years}$$

Here is one more …

$$\frac{\ln 4.45}{\ln 1.27} = 6.246 \text{ years}$$

(A secret to be revealed later!)

Up to this point there can be no doubt that these mathematical equations are correct. We have seen or used their applications at some point in our lives. Now let's explore some patterns, waves, and cycles.

It's necessary to show them to you in order to inextricably connect them with their equally important presence in waves and cycles. As we will soon discover, these constants have magical, universal qualities that play a significant role in the stock market cycles.

A transverse wave is found everywhere in day-to-day life, even though we may not always be aware of its presence. If you're alive, you are in contact with transverse waves. Your heart beating produces a transverse wave. A ripple from a stone thrown in a pond is an example of a transverse wave. Plucked strings on a guitar produce them, and the electric current from an A/C electrical outlet flows in transverse waves.

FIGURE 6.1
Transverse Wave Sine Graph

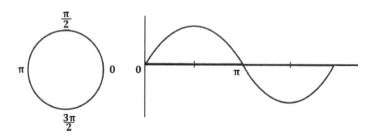

The trigonometry equation for a transverse wave is $y = \sin a$. We don't need to get into a lot of detail here about trigonometry or sines, cosines, and tangents. What I want you to notice on the graph is that each time the wave crosses the x axis, pi is present, except for at zero. Pi possesses some secret qualities, and as you will soon discover, there is more to pi than meets the eye. (I couldn't resist!) In fact, as we'll see, pi and cycles are everywhere. One cycle that every human on the planet is intimately familiar with is the circadian cycle, the human "body clock," and it is based on a twenty-four-hour cycle. It does not belong only to humans, however. Many organisms operate on the same rhythm.

How did you learn to follow the pattern? Were you taught by someone else? Did you instinctively get tired when day turned to night? Obviously, the latter is true. But why not operate on a 23.5-hour cycle? Why are humans diurnal and not nocturnal? The answers to those questions aren't important here. The point I'm trying to make is that the cycle exists. We know this for a fact. We may not be able to comprehend why or understand how it came to be, but it does exist, and so do others. I'm asking you to have an open mind to the possibility that some things do exist without our understanding why.

Many people have studied cycles, their existence, and their effect on various aspects of life. One of the more important of these people was Nikolai Kondratiev, who was a Russian economist and the first modern-day cycle theorist. He proposed that there are long economic cycles of about fifty years. According to him, a cycle starts with rising demand for goods and job creation. This is followed by rising interest rates and massive layoffs, which reduce the demand for consumer goods. Economies then contract, until confidence returns and the next upswing begins, usually accompanied by new technology. In the 1970s, increased interest in business cycles led to the rediscovery of Kondratiev's work. It was the Austrian economist Joseph Schumpeter who called these cycles Kondratiev waves and popularized them in the West. The waves were given durations of three to five years, fifteen to twenty-five years, and fifty years.

Charles Dow was one of the founders of Dow Jones and Company, as well as the first editor of the *Wall Street Journal*, where he published his ideas on the behaviour of the stock market. Considered the father of modern technical analysis in the West, his work is firmly based on cycles. He developed a theory, later called the Dow Theory, that expresses his ideas on price actions in the stock market. The Dow Theory follows six guiding principles:

1.   The market discounts all information.
2.   The market follows trends.
3.   Trends have phases.
4.   Averages must confirm each other.
5.   Volumes confirm trends.
6.   Trends continue until a reversal confirms the change.

In part, with these principles Dow recognized certain chart patterns. He then gave them names to help identify their unique formations. Although they are beyond the scope of the technical analysis covered in this book, you may be familiar with some of the patterns, which include head and shoulders, double bottoms, descending triangles, pennants, and wedges.

Ralph Nelson Elliott is known as the father of wave theory. In 1934, with the 1929 stock market crash still fresh in people's minds, Elliott began recording his observations of stock market behaviour. They came together in a general set of principles that could be applied to all degrees of wave movement in stock price charts. As he became more proficient in the application of his principles and made some necessary adjustments, their accuracy began to amaze him.

After making some impressive directional calls on the Dow to a well-respected Wall Street money manager, Elliott published his theories in 1938 in a book entitled *The Wave Principle*. By the early 1940s, Elliott had fully developed his concept of stock market behaviour, which he determined follows a progression governed by the laws of nature. Robert R. Prechter, in his introduction to *R.N. Elliott's Masterworks*, wrote this of Elliott: "He tied the patterns of collective human behaviour to the Fibonacci, or 'golden' ratio, a mathematical phenomenon known for millennia by mathematicians, scientists, artists, architects, and philosophers as one of nature's ubiquitous laws of form and progress." Elliott then put together what he considered his definitive work, *Nature's Law: The Secret of the Universe*, which was published in 1946. As a result of Elliott's ground-breaking research, thousands of institutional portfolio managers, traders, and private investors use his wave principles in their investment decisions today.

Graphing the predictions of the Elliott Wave Theory, we can observe its most basic structure. Waves 1, 3, and 5 are the primary directional movement, whereas waves 2 and 4 are countertrend deviations.

FIGURE 6.2
Elliott Wave Pattern

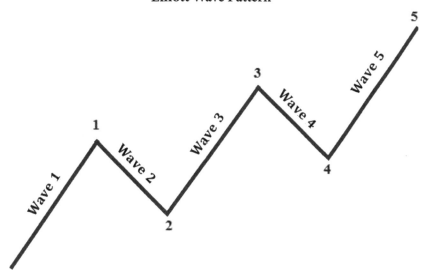

In constructing his theory of stock market behaviour, Elliott used the findings of Leonardo Fibonacci, a gifted Italian mathematician who lived in the thirteenth century. He wrote *Liber Abaci* (which means "book of calculations") and is credited with bringing Indo-Arabic numerals and the use of places in arithmetic to Europe. Fibonacci observed certain ratios of a number series that are regarded as describing the natural proportion of things in the universe. The number sequence is as follows:

$$1 + 1 + 2 + 3 + 5 + 8 + 13 + 21 + 34 + 55 + 89 + 144 + \ldots$$

The next number in the sequence is obtained by adding the two numbers preceding it.

Why are these numbers so significant? As we investigate further, we find some very interesting relationships. For example, if we divide a number in the sequence by the number following it, the result is shown in the left column of Table 6.1. If we then flip the numerator and denominator, a distinct pattern appears, as shown in the right column.

TABLE 6.1
Golden Mean

$\frac{1}{2} = 0.5$	$\frac{2}{1} = 2$
$\frac{2}{3} = 0.667$	$\frac{3}{2} = 1.5$
$\frac{3}{5} = 0.625$	$\frac{5}{3} = 1.667$
$\frac{5}{8} = 0.625$	$\frac{8}{5} = 1.6$
$\frac{8}{13} = 0.61538$	$\frac{13}{8} = 1.625$
$\frac{13}{21} = 0.61905$	$\frac{21}{13} = 1.61538$

This is just the beginning, but as the numbers get larger in the sequence, two constants emerge: 0.618 and 1.618. This relationship is known as the "golden mean." The golden mean relationship of 1 to 1.618 can be found in the workings of the universe, nature, art, music, architecture, and human anatomy. Further exploration reveals its presence in stock index and individual stock pattern price behaviour.

If we start to explore these numbers further, we arrive at what are known as Fibonacci retracement levels. Many market technicians believe that these levels represent the top or bottom of stock price movements, indicating support for a stock against a drop or resistance against a rise in a stock's price.

Besides the two retracement levels, shown on the left in Table 6.2, there are two other significant levels, shown on the right, that are derived according to the calculations shown.

TABLE 6.2
Additional Fibonacci Retracement Levels

0.618	$1 - 0.618 = 0.382$
0.50	$0.618 - 0.382 = 0.236$

The principle behind these levels is that stock price movements typically follow a saw-tooth pattern, and investors observing these patterns can identify attractive buy and sell targets.

Looking at Figure 6.3, you can see that the stock has made a significant advance from point A to point B. The retracement occurs from point B to point C, and this is where the Fibonacci retracement levels come into play. You may ask, Is it causality or self-fulfilling? Considering so many market technicians follow these levels, that question is impossible to answer. However, retracements certainly do seem to occur frequently enough to make them more than coincidental. What is impossible to determine with certainty is what level of retracement a stock will reach.

FIGURE 6.3
Basic Wave Pattern

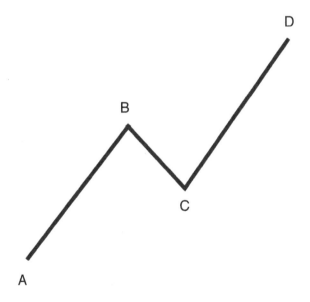

For simplicity, let us assume that this particular stock started at $0 at point A and reached $100 at point B. The retracement to point C could include any of the prices shown before the stock price advances to point D. The probability of the retracement falling within 38.2 percent and 61.8 percent is significant.

FIGURE 6.4

Fibonacci Retracement Levels

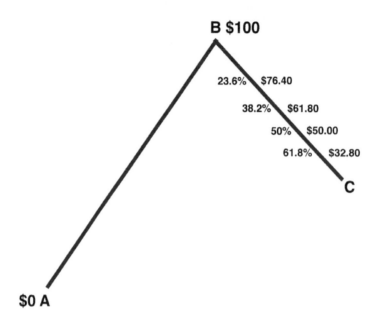

The ratio of 1:1.618 certainly has applications beyond stock price movement, and I have found the exploration of Fibonacci numbers extremely fascinating. I want to include another example for fun.

The golden rectangle in Figure 6.5 is constructed from this ratio, and derived from that is the golden spiral, a logarithmic spiral that grows by a factor of the golden ratio every quarter turn it makes. The formula for calculating the ratio is

$$1 + \frac{\sqrt{5}}{2}$$

FIGURE 6.5
The Golden Rectangle

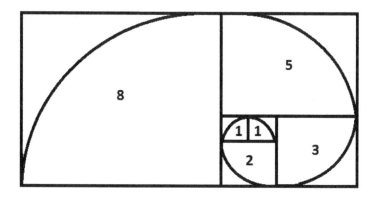

The golden rectangle can be observed in numerous works of art, including Leonardo da Vinci's *Mona Lisa* and *Vitruvian Man*. It is also said to exist in the dimensions of the Parthenon on the Acropolis. The golden spiral can be observed in a satellite image of a storm cell, the curl of an ocean wave, a nautilus shell, an atomic particle, or the shape of a galaxy.

Understanding the ebbs and flows of market waves, including Fibonacci numbers, is just another tool to have at your disposal in order to appreciate and understand the movement of markets. Knowing these levels and retracements will allow you to keep your emotions in check when you might otherwise make a rash decision, only to regret it later. Remember, making informed decisions will make you a better investor, in turn making you more money.

* * *

Although each market cycle peak and trough has its own unique set of circumstances and flashpoints, their behaviours and trajectories all follow similar, if not identical, paths. Dr. Jean-Paul Rodrigue explained these stages in a bubble in *The Geography of Transport Systems* (4th ed., Routledge, 2017). The stealth phase begins with smart money initially taking small positions. After reading the book, you may now replace "smart money" with "[Your

Name Here]." During the awareness phase, institutional money starts to enter the stock market. Remember this lesson: To make big money in the stock market, you need institutional sponsorship. The mania phase is when the public starts to enter the fray, and this is when leverage is used inappropriately to enhance returns. As the market begins to accelerate, investors increase risk exposure exactly when they should be reducing it. This phase also offers a series of "buy the dip" opportunities, until the last dip becomes a bull trap. At this point, the cycle ends and usually disappoints many emotionally drained investors who failed to understand this concept altogether.

As with all past market cycles, and, for that matter, all future cycles, one common theme emerges: this time is *not* different. When the public gets wind of how easy it is to make money in the stock market and jumps aboard, the cycle is already most likely in the mania phase. In my opinion, this is where we are in the current market cycle. There has been a huge inflow of cash into passively managed exchange-traded funds because of their low fees and relatively good performance. Easy, right? Not so fast. Remember that a rising tide lifts all boats. When the market eventually turns, which it invariably will at some point, these so-called passive long-term investors will become active sellers. In fact, in recent market sell-offs, exchange-traded funds have been larger percentage losers than the market averages themselves, indicative of what is to come.

I've presented here the top five bull markets, listed by duration (Table 6.3) and magnitude (Table 6.4). The current bull market, which began on March 9, 2009, is ranked second-longest in duration and third-largest in magnitude.

TABLE 6.3
The Top Five Bull Markets by Duration

Start	End	Duration (days)
October 12, 1990	March 24, 2000	2,075
March 9, 2009	Present (April 2016)	1,791
June 13, 1949	August 2, 1956	1,790
October 3, 1974	November 28, 1980	1,556
August 12, 1982	August 25, 1987	1,275

TABLE 6.4

The Top Five Bull Markets by Magnitude

Start	End	Magnitude
October 12, 1990	March 24, 2000	463.39%
June 13, 1949	August 2, 1956	267.08%
March 9, 2009	Present (April 2016)	249.20%
August 12, 1982	August 25, 1987	228.81%
April 28, 1942	May 29, 1946	157.70%

The purpose of interpreting a confluence of indicators, both funda-mental and technical, is to attempt to predict the future direction of the market. Knowing what the market is going to do, with a high degree of probability, before it actually happens would provide the potential for unlimited profits. Over the years a number of individuals with "black box" algorithms have claimed to be able to predict the market's direction.

Is it possible to time a market cycle to capture big gains? As with many controversial topics in investing, there is no real professional consensus on market timing. Academics claim that it's not possible, while traders and chartists swear by the idea. That said, as VisualCapitalist's Jeff Desjardins notes, one thing that everyone can probably agree on is that markets are cyclical and that securities do have recurring chart patterns. They aren't predictable all of the time, but learning the fundamentals around market cycles can help further an investor's understanding of how things work.

One person who has demonstrated a remarkable ability to forecast market cycles with incredible accuracy is an American named Martin Armstrong. His predictions have been so uncanny that he became the tar-get of a high-level government investigation. No serious market prognos-ticator has ever existed without provoking controversy, and Armstrong certainly has had his share. However, that does not take away from the fact that his forecasting ability has been incredibly accurate.

In 2014, a documentary was made based on his biography, *The Forecaster*. While it provides some insight into the man and his methods, more useful are the comments he has made in which he's publicly shared his methodology. Indeed, he has been very transparent with his forecasting model. I have personally researched his findings in great detail and have found them to be extremely compelling.

The entire theory is based on pi, the mysterious number I mentioned earlier. It essentially works like this:

$$\pi \times 1{,}000 \div 365 \text{ days} = 8.6$$

- A cycle consists of 8.6 years.
- If you divide 8.6 by 4, you get 2.15 years.
- Beginning the cycles from a reference point, you are able to create a table consisting of multiple 8.6-year cycles, with four 2.15-year intervals in between.

This is where things really begin to get interesting. If you align the intervals of past cycles with their corresponding calendar dates, you get some incredible results. Of more importance, though, is the predictions about the future that can be made based on Armstrong's observations about cycles. Whether or not you believe Armstrong's model to be true is immaterial. What is important is that this information can be used in conjunction with other tools in order to tip the scales in your favour.

There are some significant dates to be mindful of according to Armstrong's pi model, and I've provided more information on the website, www.thenextbullmarket.com. Some of Armstrong's notable predictions include Black Monday in 1987, the top of the Nikkei in 1989, the Russian debt crisis in 1998, and the housing crash in 2007.

Similar to Armstrong's model for dates of significant market inflection points, volatility has also been described as a good indicator of market inflection points. Volatility is often referred to as the "fear indicator" due to its tendency to rise in value during moments of market disruption. In 2006, volatility itself became a tradable index, and it has grown in popularity ever since. The volatility index is known as the VIX and is calculated using the price of short-dated at-the-money options on the S&P 500 index. As markets decline in value, option prices jump as investors and money managers rush to buy portfolio insurance, usually in the form of put options.

For some portfolio managers it has become the preferred choice of hedging risk. The indicator is inversely proportional to market direction. Therefore, as markets rise, volatility declines, and when markets weaken, volatility increases. This is important to remember because calls are bought when an investor is bearish on the market and puts are bought when an investor is bullish.

VOLATILITY

The volatility index, or VIX, measures the thirty-day expected volatility of the S&P 500 Index. The components of the VIX calculation are near-term put and call options on the S&P 500 with more than twenty-three days and fewer than thirty-seven days to expiration. It is regularly featured in most leading financial publications, as well as on business news channels such as BNN, CNBC, and Bloomberg TV, where the VIX is commonly referred to as the "fear index."

The benefit of the volatility index is its negative correlation to stock market returns. Where other asset classes, such as gold or real estate, may offer some diversification from stock market fluctuations, the VIX is a pure risk-mitigation tool. As such, it is widely used by retail investors, institutional traders, and hedge funds. The premise is simple: when market indices advance, volatility drops, and when market indices fall, volatility spikes higher.

I also refer to the VIX as the "greed index." As markets climb higher for extended periods of time with no significant pullbacks, the volatility index will trend lower. Just as spikes in volatility can indicate temporary market bottoms, low volatility readings can indicate interim market tops. Therefore, it is possible to use high and low volatility levels to make both buying and selling decisions.

The all-time low for the index was recorded on December 22, 1993, at 9.31, and the all-time high was hit on November 20, 2008, at 80.86. The low VIX level in December 1993 would have signalled a sell, which would have kept you out of the biggest technology rally in history. The buy signal in November 2008 would have got you into the current seven-year bull market four months before the market bottomed in March 2009. If you observed the inflection points at which the index reached highs of at least 40, you would see that almost all of these occurrences signalled excellent buying opportunities. As with the signal in December 1993, similar observations have shown that low volatility can indicate a sell signal far too early, suggesting that the VIX is a far better buy indicator than a sell indicator.

FIGURE 6.6

VIX and S&P 500 Indexes

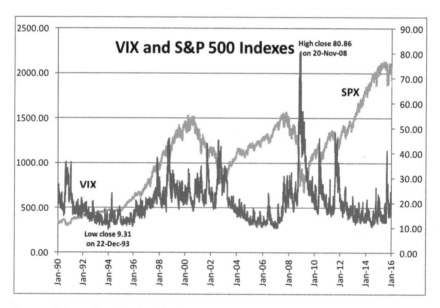

Source: Chicago Board Options Exchange

Expanding on the theme that the VIX indicates a buy above the 40 level, Table 6.5 shows a list of occurrences when it came close to or reached 40.

TABLE 6.5
VIX Closing Highs

Date	VIX	S&P
August 23, 1990	36.47	307.06
October 30, 1997	38.20	903.68
October 8, 1998	45.74	959.44
September 20, 2001	43.74	984.54
August 5, 2002	45.08	834.60
October 7, 2002	42.64	785.28
November 20, 2008	80.86	752.44
May 20, 2010	45.79	1,071.59
August 8, 2011	48.00	1,119.46
August 24, 2015	40.74	1,893.21

Comparing the VIX buy indicator with the corresponding chart, only one circumstance did not indicate a suitable time to buy. That was on September 20, 2001, or shortly after September 11, 2001. If you had bought after the World Trade Center attack, you would have suffered a loss of 20 percent for another year until October 7, 2002. Furthermore, the attack occurred when the technology bubble was still crashing, and the crash was just starting to gain momentum in November 2000. Risk-averse investors may have determined that the correction had not run its full course, which may have prevented them from jumping back in too soon.

* * *

In an attempt to cover subjects that are not well known to retail investors or that are frequently mentioned in technical analysis material, I've discussed a number of patterns, waves, and cycles that seem to make sense to a lot of sophisticated investors. Rather than going into the subject in any great depth, my purpose was to introduce to you market indicators that are out of the scope of most mainstream media business subject matter and to provide you with additional ammunition for making informed investment decisions.

As you may already be aware, there are two schools of thought when it comes to stock analysis. One believes that fundamental analysis is the only thing that matters, and one believes that technical analysis is the only thing that matters. This polarized thinking is counter-productive, and in order to balance the book and not appear one-sided, which I'm not, I have included the following chapter on fundamental analysis. My approach to fundamental analysis is similar to that of this technical chapter, as I approach the subject from a more practical angle in terms of explanation and understanding.

7

FUNDAMENTAL ANALYSIS

If you are an investor who is intimidated by annual reports, fear no more — you are about to be amazed! I'm about to unlock the secrets of the balance sheet and earnings statement and explain them in easy-to-understand terms. If you can do basic math on the back of an envelope, you will have no problem interpreting the financials of any company you are interested in. It will also teach you, on the other hand, to determine which ones to keep your hard-earned money far away from.

FUNDAMENTAL ANALYSIS DEMYSTIFIED

Let's start with the balance sheet. This is where the information about a company's assets, liabilities, and owners' (or shareholders') equity is found. Assets include cash, inventory, property, buildings, equipment, intangibles, and goodwill. Liabilities include, but are not limited to, accounts payable and short- and long-term debt. Owners' equity typically includes retained earnings, paid-in capital, and perhaps some other smaller items.

The earnings statement is where the cash transactions of a company are represented. Usually the first item on the earnings statement is revenue, or how much the company made in a given calendar year. Revenue is followed by the cost of goods sold, operating expenses, depreciation, interest income, interest expense, earnings before tax, and income tax expenses. After subtracting all expenses from the revenue, the result is the company's profit or loss. If the company has made a profit, the final line item is the net earnings (income).

TABLE 7.1

Sample Balance Sheet and Earnings Statement

	Balance Sheet			Statement of Earnings	
	Assets		Item 4	Revenue	**16.5**
	Cash			Cost of goods sold	7
	Inventory			Operating expenses	**6.5**
	Intangibles			Depreciation	
	Goodwill			Interest income	
	Property, buildings, equipment			Interest expense	
Item 1	**Total Assets**	10.5	Item 5	Earnings before tax	3
	Liabilities and Equity			Income tax expense	1
	Accounts payable		Item 6	Net earnings	2
	Short-term debt				
	Long-term debt				
Item 2	**Total Liabilites**	5.5			
	Owner's equity				
	Retained earnings				
Item 3	Total Owner's Equity	5			

Notice that my balance sheet contains only three data points. The reason for this is to demonstrate its symmetry. All balance sheets must balance, no pun intended. The equation to represent this is assets = liabilities + owners' equity. Therefore, assets – liabilities = owners' equity, and it does.

The statement of earnings is straightforward as well. It should be clear that earnings before tax (Item 5) = revenue (Item 4) – (cost of goods + expenses). Subtracting the income tax expense (taxes payable) from earnings before tax is equal to the net earnings (Item 6). Easy, right?

Now, what we are able to do with these numbers is really exciting. So let's get started. First, we want to make sure that a company will remain solvent. To do this we need to determine the amount of financial leverage (debt) a company has on its balance sheet. Too much debt is bad; just enough is fine. I will discuss excessive debt in more detail later.

One of the commonly used measures of the size of a company's debt is the debt-to-equity ratio. It is calculated by dividing debt by the owners' equity and is expressed as a percentage. To keep things simple, I did not list the debt on the balance sheet above, but I will provide the amount here: 2.

$$\text{Debt-to-Equity} = \frac{\text{Debt}}{\text{Owner's Equity}} = \frac{2}{5} \times 100 = 40 \text{ percent}$$

Although different levels of debt are considered acceptable for a company depending on the type of industry it operates in, generally speaking total debt should not be more than 50 percent of equity. This ratio can serve as a warning that borrowing is excessive. Essentially, the higher the ratio, the higher the financial risk. However, even a ratio as high as 150 percent would not be unheard of for a utility company, and the leverage would still not be considered unreasonable.

Another measure of a company's debt load is its liquidity. To determine that, we can use the working capital ratio. It is calculated by dividing a company's current assets (Item 1) by its current liabilities (Item 2). (I have used total assets and total liabilities for ease.)

$$\text{Working Capital} = \frac{\text{Current Assets}}{\text{Current Liabilities}} = \frac{10.5}{5.5} = 1.9$$

A working capital ratio of 2 is considered satisfactory, since such a level indicates that a company would likely have cash on hand to pay for any short-term needs and, as a result, would not likely need to resort to selling illiquid inventory in order to raise cash. A working capital ratio of 5 or greater could be an indication of poor sales or excessive inventory.

Checking off the list, we now know that the company is solvent and not in danger of having to declare bankruptcy, and that it is liquid enough to handle any adverse short-term obligations. Also, we know the company is profitable, since it reported net earnings of 2. The next ratios will determine how profitable.

The net profit margin is calculated by dividing the net earnings (Item 6) by the revenue (Item 4). This figure is stated as a percentage.

$$\text{Net Profit Margin} = \frac{\text{Net Earnings}}{\text{Revenue}} = \frac{2}{16.5} \times 100 = 12 \text{ percent}$$

The net profit margin does not really have a lot of significance on its own, but it can be used when comparing year-over-year earnings or two separate companies to one another. A higher trending net profit margin over time is a good indicator of management's ability to run the business well.

The return on equity (ROE) is another gauge of management's ability. A higher ROE indicates that management is doing a good job of investing the common shareholders' capital. It is calculated by dividing the net earnings (Item 6) by the owners' equity (Item 3) and is expressed as a percentage. Canadian banks typically have an ROE in the mid-teens. A return on equity of 40 percent is considered outstanding.

$$\text{Return on Equity} = \frac{\text{Net Earnings}}{\text{Owner's Equity}} = \frac{2}{5} \times 100 = 40 \text{ percent}$$

Earnings per share are easily calculated by dividing net earnings (Item 6) by the number of common shares outstanding. The common shares outstanding can be found in the owners' equity. In order to keep the ratios normalized with net earnings of 2, use the common shares' outstanding adjustment factor of 0.769. (Note: Large-number rounding required adjusting the denominator in order to provide corresponding answers.) The common share market price is $80 per share.

$$\text{Earnings per Share} = \frac{\text{Net Earnings}}{\text{Common Outstanding}} = \frac{2}{0.769} = \$2.60$$

$$\text{Price Earnings Ratio (P/E)} = \frac{\text{Market Price}}{\text{Earnings per Share}} = \frac{\$80}{\$2.60} = 30.8$$

The price earnings ratio tells investors how expensive a stock is relative to the market as a whole or its peers. It is very subjective and may or may not be justified depending on the quality of a company's earnings or its growth rate.

If a company pays a dividend, the dividend payable is able to provide two important pieces of information: how sustainable the dividend is likely to be and what the dividend yield is. The dividend payout ratio is calculated by dividing the dividend payable by the net income (Item 6). In order to keep the ratio normalized with net earnings of 2, use the dividend payable adjustment factor of 0.80. The result should be expressed as a percentage.

$$\text{Dividend Payout Ratio} = \frac{\text{Dividend Payable}}{\text{Net Income}} = \frac{0.80}{2} \times 100 = 40 \text{ percent}$$

A dividend payout of less than 40 percent is considered conservative and means the dividend is easily covered. Canadian bank payouts are about 50 percent.

The dividend yield is calculated by dividing the dividend payable by the common shares outstanding and is expressed as a percentage.

$$\text{Dividend Yield} = \frac{\text{Dividend Payable}}{\text{Common Outstanding}} = \frac{0.80}{0.769} = 1.04 \text{ percent}$$

If you prefer, the dividend payout and dividend yield can be calculated on a per share basis since we know the earnings per share (net income), the market price per share (common outstanding), and dividend per share (dividend payable), all of which can be easily found in the annual report or on any financial website.

Now that we know how to evaluate a balance sheet and earnings statement, we need to determine if the numbers add up. No one can detect fraud until it is too late if a company decides to act outside the law. Unless, of course, you're Harry Markopolos. Remember him? Markopolos was the forensic accountant who finally uncovered that Bernie Madoff was running a Ponzi scheme. Markopolos said that he knew within five minutes that Madoff's numbers didn't add up. It took him another four hours to mathematically prove that they could have only been obtained by fraud.

Incidentally, a major contributor to his evidence was the options market. Madoff claimed that the investment returns from his fund were made from option writing. Markopolos knew, based on the alleged amount of money being managed, which was in the billions, that in order to produce the kinds of returns Madoff was claiming, an enormous quantity of options would have to have been traded. What Markopolos did was brilliant. He contacted every option market maker that could have handled the size of order flow that would have been required and asked one simple question: "Do you do any option trading with Madoff?" Well, you know the rest of the story.

There is an unlimited number of ways to produce aggressive accounting. In most cases, they never materialize into a problem. However, in a small number of cases they do. If a company is being up-front and disclosing all material financial information, there are certain red flags that can warn investors of potential danger. These red flags typically are found in three areas: assets, expenses, and revenue recognition.

The first red flag is the quality of assets. A very popular strategy for companies looking to grow is the acquisition of higher-growth companies. When money is cheap, like today, many company execs decide it is a good time to binge. This is accomplished by issuing debt and paying a large premium for the company being bought. As a result, the acquirer has to offset the debt (liability) on the balance sheet with an asset. In most cases, the assets of the acquired company do not offset the debt used for the purchase. Therefore, it is recorded as goodwill.

Each year goodwill is tested for impairment; under certain guidelines, if the assets are deemed non-performing, the test results in a non-cash charge against earnings. Look at this equation again:

Assets = Liabilities + Owner's Equity

If liabilities grow significantly because of an excessive amount of debt, the only way to balance the equation is to increase assets. Therefore, if goodwill and intangibles make up a high percentage of the assets, be very cautious.

TABLE 7.2
Components of the Balance Sheet

	Balance Sheet	
	Assets	
	Cash	
	Inventory	
	Intangibles	
	Goodwill	
	Property, buildings, equipment	
Item 1	**Total Assets**	10.5

Expenses are the second potential red flag. Recall that, in the statement of earnings, the equation for earnings before tax is revenue – (cost of goods + expenses). By deferring expenses, earnings can be artificially inflated.

TABLE 7.3
Components of the Earnings Statement

	Statement of Earnings	
Item 4	Revenue	16.5
	Cost of goods sold	7
	Operating expenses	6.5
	Depreciation	
	Interest income	
	Interest expense	
Item 5	Earnings before tax	3

The third red flag that investors should be on the lookout for, relating to revenue, is by far the most widely abused. Revenue recognition is an accounting principle, and it relates to the way in which a company determines how its sales become recognized as revenue. The accounting methods a company uses to report its finances can be found in the footnotes to its statements. Since companies can manipulate the timing of when they submit their financials for reporting and when they receive payments, certain accounting procedures have been put in place to govern the adjustments necessary and ensure that these discrepancies in timing are accounted for. However, if a company is purposely being deceptive, it can employ tactics to inflate revenue or defer expenses. Other mechanisms for misrepresenting income involve recording revenue before goods are delivered or negotiating barter arrangements to generate sales.

Congratulations! Not only have you learned a great deal about fundamental analysis, you have actually analyzed a real company. The example provided was Starbucks, from its 2014 annual report. You can get the full document on www.thenextbullmarket.com. For the material referenced above, please see pages 45, 47, 48, and 51 of the report. (Note: Results are not exact due to large-number rounding.)

Now that you have the basic tools for understanding companies' financial reports, it's time to learn how to use them in order to do the research necessary to make sound investment choices. I know that there are lots of financial advisors out there who will offer to do this work for you — and make no mistake, the advice of a good financial advisor is very valuable — but there's still no substitute for doing your own investment research. Here's what Warren Buffett has to say on the subject:

> There's no need to get an MBA in bean counting, but a basic understanding of company accountancy procedures and balance sheet reading is a must. There's a lot of smoke and mirrors in the investment world, and many an annual report is designed to deceive, not clarify. Be on your toes for these shenanigans, at least by being able to comprehend the game they're playing.
>
> While it's true that your stockbroker should be able to offer some sensible advice, remember he or she probably

has neither the time nor the inclination to dig deep. There simply is no substitute for your own spadework.

— Warren Buffett, from *Thoughts of Chairman Buffett* by Simon Reynolds

So let's have a look at how you can get the necessary financial information in order to make sound investing choices.

DO-IT-YOURSELF RESEARCH

As I mentioned in the introduction, one of the main features of this book is that it offers an investment plan designed to help you protect your assets and make money in the market. I will be providing details of this plan a bit later. For the time being, though, I will simply make reference to it in a general way. I want to go over the general rules of what you need to do before we get into the finer points.

When you have bought the investments in The Plan, it will be very important for you to closely follow the twenty companies' financial health and monitor their progress through the next bull market cycle. The reporting that will be of particular interest includes earnings announcements, records of dividends, buybacks, mergers, annual meetings, annual reports, share splits, special dividends, and any other materially relevant information.

Luckily, the internet has made it extremely easy to research and find this type of information. Most publicly traded companies now do a very good job of providing investor-related material on their own websites. They may even have a dedicated portal for investor relations. Companies may provide downloadable material from recent corporate events, in PowerPoint, that contain pertinent information on quarterly financials, or company projections in simple language with graphical support. Additionally, research analysts, whose responsibility it is to cover a particular company, may be listed as a source of research material on the corporate website. Many companies now allow interested parties to subscribe to their email services. Companies may have a list of items that investors can choose to have emailed straight to them as soon as the corporate-related news or press releases are distributed. I have also listed all The Plan company websites in the SWOT (strengths, weaknesses, opportunities, threats) analysis profiles in the Appendix. As an added convenience, I have aggregated the corporate information from all the companies in The Plan, and I provide regular updates at www.thenextbullmarket.com.

Apart from the information provided by the companies themselves, there is also a tremendous amount of third-party research available online. Now, not all of this is of the same quality. For example, I do not give a lot of credibility to research produced by firms whose analysts cover a company on the one hand and have a relationship with that company's corporate finance department on the other. Hardly unbiased. Therefore, I try to select research that has no other purpose than providing sound, objective advice. Short, concise, informative write-ups can be found on websites such as The Motley Fool (www.fool.com) and Seeking Alpha (www.seekingalpha.com). The Google and Yahoo finance portals also do a good job of informing users of upcoming calendar events, such as earnings releases and dividend announcements.

Unfortunately, for Canadians investors and Canadian publicly traded companies, third-party unbiased research is more difficult to find than it is for U.S.-based companies. Subscription-based services are available, one of which is 5i Research. However, because the bigger brokerage houses all flog the same large Canadian publicly traded companies, 5i seems to focus its efforts on smaller, more obscure Canadian companies.

Depending on where you reside, another excellent source of public company information may be your local library. In the Greater Toronto Area, online accessibility of databases and catalogues has made this resource very useful and quite robust. If a specific company is being researched, then the information available is limitless.

The number of online magazines, newspapers, and journals that offer useful corporate and economic information is huge — too numerous to list here. When using these tools for research, start by narrowing down your search using the most popular business-related publications first, such as the *Globe & Mail* or *National Post*. The Canadian Business and Current Affairs Database aggregates articles written on all business-related matters in a host of publications. The *Financial Post* Advisor provides corporate snapshots, investor reports, information on fixed-income securities and preferred shares, details of mergers and acquisitions, and much more. Mergent Online offers among all of its services a corporate calendar of upcoming earnings announcements. Value Line also offers a concise, unbiased, one-page research report on most U.S.-based corporations. Regrettably, only a select few large Canadian companies are covered.

THE DIVIDEND CONUNDRUM

Income-oriented investors are very focused on yield and often fail to look at the bigger picture. This narrow-minded thinking can sometimes lead to unfortunate circumstances, especially this late in the market cycle. Investors in the energy sector, which tends to attract yield seekers because of its high-yielding stocks, have been hit particularly hard since the collapse of commodity prices starting in 2015.

High-yielding stocks are typically found in the financial, consumer staple, energy, telecom, utility, and REIT (real estate investment trust) sectors. In times of market volatility, these sectors are the ones that typically demonstrate their lower beta (volatility). So, why is there a tendency for investors to seek what are perceived to be "safer" high-yielding stocks in the latter stages of the business cycle? Because of the conviction that the yield will cushion, or create a floor underneath, the stock price. What is overlooked or simply ignored is the fact that, when a correction does occur, even high-yielding stocks will experience a considerable depreciation in price. Thereafter, depending on the economic climate, the dividend may have to be cut to strengthen the balance sheet, precisely what happened to the energy patch in 2015.

So, how do you determine if a company you own stock in may need to cut its dividend? This can be discovered by examining the company's dividend payout ratio, which is a simple formula for calculating if the stock you own or are considering is capable of sustaining its dividend. It is calculated by dividing the dividend payable to common shareholders by the net income. On a per share basis it is calculated by dividing the dividend per share by the earnings per share. In both cases it is then multiplied by one hundred and shown as a percentage.

$$\text{Dividend Payout Ratio} = \frac{\text{Dividend to Common Shareholders}}{\text{Net Income}} \times 100$$

Depending on the industry or sector, the payout ratio can be used as an indicator to determine if the dividend is at risk. For example, a bank stock with a payout of 50 percent would be considered conservative. On the other hand, a utility stock or REIT could have a payout of close to 100 percent and may still be relatively safe. Each industry or sector must be gauged on its own merits, comparables, and guidelines. However, if the dividend payout ratio were to exceed 100 percent, the dividends would have to be taken out of retained earnings, depleting the shareholders' equity. Over the long term, this scenario would be unsustainable and the dividend would eventually have to be reduced or suspended. When this occurs, usually the common shares experience a significant drop in price.

A comparison of The Plan constituents I have selected, ranked by performance and then by yield in Table 7.4, clearly demonstrates that high-yielding stocks do not perform as well as lower-yielding stocks. In theory this makes sense, since a portion of earnings are paid out to shareholders as dividends, instead of being used to reinvest in and grow the business. Another way of expressing this comparison is by classifying all twenty of these stocks as either growth or value stocks.

TABLE 7.4
Plan Companies Listed by Performance and Yield

Name	Rank	Yield
Alimentation Couche-Tard Inc.	1	0.51
Starbucks Corporation	2	1.53
Magna International Inc.	3	1.24
Apple Inc.	4	1.64
Capital One Financial Corp.	5	1.83
Walt Disney Co.	6	1.29
Novo Nordisk	7	1.30
MasterCard Inc.	8	0.81
Canadian Pacific Railway	9	0.68

Name	Rank	Yield
The Home Depot Inc.	10	2.15
Nike Inc.	11	1.24
Boeing Co.	12	3.06
Brookfield Asset Management Inc.	13	1.11
Canadian Tire Corporation	14	1.59
Costco Wholesale Corp.	15	1.17
Enbridge Inc.	16	3.80
Toronto Dominion Bank	17	3.76
Telus Corporation	18	4.28
National Bank	19	4.44
Royal Bank	20	4.04

I understand that income-oriented investors may require the income from dividend-paying stocks in their portfolios to pay for monthly expenses. The good news is that you don't have to sacrifice growth for yield. There is another option available.

You can simply harvest profits from the best performers in the portfolio and have them paid out the same way you would receive dividends on a quarterly basis. This strategy serves two purposes: it pays you an income on a tax preferential basis (capital gains versus dividends) and it assists in automatically rebalancing your portfolio. This should only be done in a fee-based account, where no commissions apply.

I'd like to look at an actual example of a high dividend–paying stock to demonstrate the power of this concept. The Royal Bank is currently trading at $75 and pays a quarterly dividend of $0.81. Multiplying $0.81 by four and dividing that number by $75 produces a yield of 4.3 percent. During the next correction, RBC should drop to approximately $37.50, meaning that it would be trading at about a 50 percent discount to its current price. Don't believe me? Look at my target price in The Plan, in Chapter 9. It fell to $35.25 in 2009. All the Canadian banks lost approximately 50 percent of their value during the last two market corrections. If the price of RBC drops by 50 percent in the next correction, then the yield would double to 8.6 percent. If you were to purchase the stock at $37.50, the odds of you doubling your money would be very good. Plus, you would get an added bonus. Applying the Rule of 72 to the 8.6 percent dividend yield, you would double your money again in 8.5 years. Unless, of course, RBC has to cut its coveted dividend, which no Canadian bank has risked doing in a very long time.

Now, the relationship between yield and performance does not apply only to individual companies. It can be seen in the market as a whole also. The diagram in Figure 7.1 illustrates the dividend yield on the S&P 500 since 1900. What this demonstrates is that the dividend yield is inversely correlated to the level of the S&P 500. In other words, when the market is overvalued, stock yields are low and vice versa. It also suggests that when yields are high, the market is priced at a discount and stocks should be bought.

FIGURE 7.1
S&P Dividend Yield

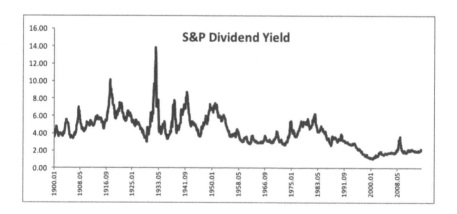

Source: Robert J. Schiller, *Irrational Exuberance*

In the last generation, you can see that the S&P dividend yield spiked in 1991, 2003, and again in 2009. Those were all great entry points to buy equities. Currently, the yield on the S&P 500 is at 2.11 percent. This extremely low dividend yield is another indication that the market is overvalued.

I am compelled to discuss another matter regarding dividends. Lately, Bay and Wall Street experts have been touting the benefits of owning a company's higher-yielding common shares over their respective bonds because of the paltry coupons. Their rationale for this flawed recommendation is that the dividend yield on many familiar stocks is 1 percent higher than on their debt, on a pre-tax basis. Listed below are the ten highest yielding stocks on the Dow and their projected dividend payout ratios.

TABLE 7.5
The Dow Jones Industrials' Top Ten Highest Yielding Stocks

Company/Ticker	Recent Price	Div Yield	Market Value (billions)	1-Yr Total Return	Projected 2016 Payout Ratio*
Chevron/CVX	$94.84	4.6%	$178.0	−7.1%	310%
Verizon Communications/VZ	53.52	4.2	218.4	14.3	57
Caterpillar/CAT	75.22	4.1	43.8	−3.8	84
Pfizer/PFE	32.93	3.8	203.9	−1.2	52
Cisco Systems/CSCO	28.00	3.8	140.9	6.3	40
ExxonMobil/XOM	83.31	3.6	346.0	1.4	123
International Business Machines/IBM	150.02	3.5	144.2	−4.1	38
Boeing/BA	127.93	3.4	83.3	−12.8	51
Merck/MRK	55.63	3.4	154.4	0.6	49
Intel/INTC	32.08	3.3	151.3	6.6	45

All data as of April 6, 2016

*As portion of expected 2016 earnings

Source: FactSet/Barron's

A couple of issues come to mind as I examine this chart. First, if you had purchased Chevron, Caterpillar, IBM, or Boeing one year earlier for the yield, you wouldn't have made any money. Second, the payout ratio of Chevron, Caterpillar, and Exxon looks questionable. I'm not suggesting that any of these companies will have to cut their dividend, especially Exxon, but why tempt fate?

If you were to purchase the bonds of any of these companies, I would be willing to say with a high degree of conviction that you would get your principal back at maturity. However, if you bought the common shares for the 1 percent pick-up in yield, I don't believe that would be a good trade-off. When the next correction happens, we could expect these stocks to drop somewhere between 30 percent and 50 percent. Given that, the bottom line is you would be waiting a long time to recoup your losses, and the opportunity cost would be tremendous.

DERIVATIVES: FINANCIAL WEAPONS OF MASS DESTRUCTION

I deliberated a great deal about whether to include this topic in the book, and after careful consideration, I decided that it was necessary to do so, since derivatives were responsible for the last financial crisis and will most likely play a part in the next.

Derivatives are ubiquitous, especially in banking. So, whether you are aware of them or not, the institution you use for your banking needs most likely employs them as a part of its business practice. Using our newly acquired fundamental analysis skills, we can determine who has exposure on their balance sheet and if we as customers are at risk. While risk is always an issue where money is concerned, Canadians are better protected than citizens of many countries. Oversight of derivative exposure by financial institutions in Canada is monitored by the Office of the Superintendent of Financial Institutions (OSFI). Fortunately, our banks in Canada are somewhat more conservative in both management practice and regulation and have avoided most of the recent global financial catastrophes as a result of their misuse.

So, what are derivatives and why do they exist in the first place? Although they can be used to speculate on any segment of the financial markets, they are commonly used for a prosaic and quite legitimate purpose, which is to reduce risk. Usually they are used when significant amounts of money are at stake. As a result, the size of the transactions involved is usually very large, and the business is also very profitable.

Whenever there is any business activity that produces sizable profits for financial institutions, there is a tendency for them to underestimate the magnitude of the inherent risks associated with the activity and to simply leverage their balance sheets. This tendency is encouraged since there is a presumption among derivatives traders that risks can be reduced or eliminated substantially by offsetting positions against one another using a technique known as "netting."

However, as we will see, while this may be true in theory, in reality there is always a breaking point. The breaking point occurs when one or more parties (also known as counterparties) overextend their capacity to fulfill their obligation (they take on too much leverage) and default on their commitments. This ultimately sets off a chain reaction that brings forth massive losses.

To understand the scope of the money involved, let's begin with some numbers we are more familiar with. In Canada, our national debt is about $1.3 trillion. In the United States, the national debt is about $18.4 trillion. Economists believe that as a country's debt increases relative to its GDP, greater stress is placed on the respective society. Canada's current GDP figure is about $1.8 trillion, which means that its debt-to-GDP ratio now stands at about 72 percent. The U.S. GDP is about $18 trillion, so its debt-to-GDP ratio has just exceeded 100 percent. Lately, individual Canadians' personal debt-to-disposable income ratio has been reported to have reached 164 percent, a figure that some argue is unsustainable.

Now that we have established the enormity of a trillion dollars, it is estimated that global derivative exposure is currently around $600 trillion in notional value. This number is higher, not lower, than the outstanding notional value of what existed before the last financial crisis.

To put this into context, that's more than thirty-eight times the U.S. national debt.

Keep in mind, the notional value is not the total amount at risk. The amount at risk is a function of the notional value change, as a result of change in interest rates, foreign currency, credit default, et cetera, where the loss is borne. Put another way, the total gain or loss is a result of each variable (interest rate, currency, default) outcome or influence on the notional value. The formal definition is the difference between the spot price and a given reference point.

Here's an example of how this works in practice. Assume a sovereign wealth fund owns $100 million in a particular bond issue. It would like to protect the interest rate exposure (rising interest rates lower bond prices), so it enters into an agreement with a dealer that allows it to fix the interest rate of the bond returns. How interest rates behave between the initiation of the contract and the expiration will determine the dealers' profit or loss. The sovereign wealth fund will receive the fixed rate throughout the contract period.

As you can see, determining loss of the notional value is extremely difficult because it is based on the outcome of a future event (rising interest rates, currency fluctuations, debt default). Also note that one party's loss is the other party's gain — it's a zero-sum transaction.

So, one may ask, is it possible for the potential loss to be calculated as a percent of the notional value? The answer is difficult to determine because the reporting agencies disclose information differently, and, to my knowledge, no one has been able to predict the future. However, it is easy to assess that a 10 percent loss of value in the overall derivatives market would be equal to a $60 trillion decline. A 1 percent loss would be equal to $6 trillion. A tenth of a 1 percent loss would be equal to $600 billion. Coincidentally, this is approximately equal to what the cost of the financial crisis bail-out was in 2008–2009. Give or take $100 billion.

An event that would likely cause another financial crisis of that scope is referred to in the industry as "tail risk," or a "black swan" — a term that refer to the low statistical probability of an event occurring based on the standard deviation. Tail risk refers to an outlier event (the ends) on a bell curve that mathematically has only a small chance of happening. As we have experienced in the past, however remote mathematically, these black swan events continue to reoccur. According to James Rickards, advisor to the Department of Defense and the Pentagon, this can be attributed to the fact that the protective measures are based on flawed risk models and complex structures that cannot be easily measured.

Another moniker used to describe the possibility of continued market collapses after 2007 was the "Minsky moment." The mathematician-turned-economist Hyman Minsky described the three stages of a debt financing model that changed throughout an economic cycle. He proposed that as an economy strengthens, a firm's temptation to take on more debt becomes irresistible. Banks add to the dynamic by lowering their credit standards. The longer a boom lasts, the more unstable the financial system grows, ultimately leading to a financial crisis. So the question on everyone's mind is, "When is the next Minsky moment?"

The European derivative reporting agency is the Bank for International Settlements (BIS). It reports an aggregate of over-the-counter derivatives for financial institutions, so it is difficult to determine what the exposure is on an individual company basis. It shouldn't be a surprise that 80 percent of the outstanding derivatives today are interest-rate-related, according to the BIS.

In the United States, the Office of the Comptroller of the Currency (OCC) reports on U.S. financial company derivative exposure. It does a much better job of reporting derivative exposure on an individual company basis.

As previously mentioned, the Canadian reporting agency is the Superintendent of Financial Institutions (OSFI). Canadian financial institutions are not immune to participating in the derivatives market, and Table 7.6 has a list of banks' derivative exposure in Canada.

TABLE 7.6
Derivatives Held by Canadian Banks

	Notional Amount 2016 Q1 (Trillions)	
	Contracts Held for Trading Purposes	Total Contracts
Bank of Montreal	4,674,494,120	4,687,344,075
Bank of Nova Scotia	4,493,072,882	5,049,724,525
CIBC	2,057,501,664	2,413,013,684
National Bank	783,225,008	927,023,226
Royal Bank	12,234,181,782	12,424,920,150
TD Bank	6,492,847,582	7,630,197,455

Source: OSFI

Global leaders have recognized the fragility of our financial system. As a result, a new mechanism has been created to provide liquidity and stability to the world's markets in the event of another financial crisis. The International Monetary Fund has been given the authority to print a kind of currency — known as Special Drawing Rights — that would be accepted globally. The ability of countries to use this tool should ensure that the world does not come to an end as a result of the next disaster du jour.

Banks around the world that pose a risk to the stability of the global financial system have been given the designation of G-SIBs, or global systemically important banks. They include banks in the United States, Europe, and Asia. Although the Royal Bank was given consideration, none of the Canadian banks were bestowed with the designation.

Since the financial crisis of 2008, a number of banks outside of North America have not been able to get their houses in order. In fact, some have gotten progressively worse. One bank in particular has caught the attention of the International Monetary Fund (IMF). Since 2007, its stock price has fallen over 90 percent from US$159 to US$14 in mid-2016. The bank I am referring to is Deutsche Bank.

On closer inspection, Deutsche Bank has on its balance sheet a notional derivative exposure of about US$46 trillion. To put that into perspective, it is close to 1.5 times the amount of Lehman Brothers' exposure was just before it imploded back in 2008. The IMF has recently issued a statement saying that Deutsche Bank poses the greatest risk to the global financial system. It seems that Deutsche Bank is not alone, as Italian, Spanish, and Greek banks are also in desperate need of cash. Well-capitalized banks, like the ones in Canada, require capital reserves at a minimum of 10.5 percent under Basel III, introduced in 2013. Deutsche Bank's reserve is below 3 percent, exactly where Lehman's was before it went bankrupt.

In other words, it seems that banks in Europe are up to the same old tricks again. They accept money from depositors who trust they will keep it safe for them. Instead, those same banks take enormously risky bets, and when things blow up, taxpayers are on the hook to bail them out.

BOND KINGS

It is believed in the investment community that bond traders are smarter than equity traders. I don't know if that is necessarily true, but the bond market is usually "tipped off" for potential trouble before the equity market becomes aware of any problems. One of the tip-offs of a deteriorating market cycle is the credit quality of debt being issued. As investors search for higher yields, underwriting firms are only too willing to issue the debt of companies with weaker balance sheets. This has begun to occur with greater frequency today. Two other key indicators that raise suspicion about deteriorating economic conditions are spreads and default rates.

What are spreads? A spread is the difference in yield when comparing two different bonds. Comparisons can be made between bonds with different maturities, credit quality, or country of origin. For instance, the spread between a Government of Canada ten-year bond (1.3 percent) and a thirty-year bond (2 percent) is currently 0.7 percent, or 70 basis points (2 to 1.3 percent). The spread between a Government of Canada five-year bond (0.75 percent) and a five-year corporate bond (8.25 percent) is 7.5 percent (8.25 to 0.75 percent). The spread between a Government of Canada ten-year bond (1.3 percent) and a German ten-year bund (0.2 percent) is 1.1 percent (1.3 to 0.2 percent).

The change in percent (basis points) between different credit quality bonds can indicate how well an economy is functioning. For the last six years, spreads between Canadian government and corporate bonds have traded within 3 and 4 percent (300 to 400 basis points), a sign of economic stability, or at least complacency. However, more recently, spreads have begun to widen (deteriorate). So the question becomes, what do widening spreads imply? As spreads begin to widen, especially between government bonds (which are risk-free) and high-yield bonds (which are riskier), the implication is that investors are expecting a greater return for putting their capital at risk. In periods of economic instability, such as an economic slowdown, riskier bonds produce higher yields and risk-free bonds lower (flight to quality). As of the end of February 2016, the one-year return for the Canadian-dollar-hedged Markit iBoxx USD Liquid High Yield index was down 8.26 percent.

Another disturbing sign is the influx of redemptions in the high-yield market, which is causing it to seize up. The illiquid market has forced managers to sell at below market prices, exacerbating losses. Currently, the spread between high-yield debt and GOC bonds has increased to around 7.5 percent, or 750 basis points. According to bond traders, this spread indicates a 50 percent probability of a recession. During the recessions of 1990 and 2001, spreads widened to about 10 percent, or 1,000 basis points. In the recession of 2008, the spread exploded to 20 percent, or 2,000 basis points.

FIGURE 7.3
Spread Between High-Yield Debt and U.S. Government Bonds

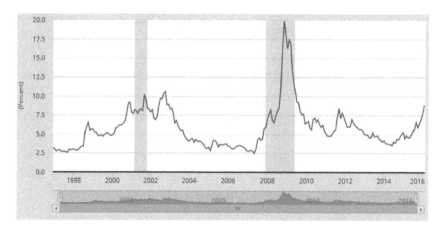

Source: BofA Merrill Lynch; St. Louis Federal Reserve

When a company's debt becomes distressed, the likelihood of default increases. When default rates begin to increase, the probability of a recession also increases. Default rates are an indication of a weakening economic climate. As growth begins to slow, companies' profits deteriorate, and they eventually find it more difficult to repay their debt obligations. The default rate of the past three recessions for high-yield debt has averaged between 8 and 16 percent. Currently, the 2016 U.S. high-yield default rate forecast has jumped to 4.5 percent according to Fitch Ratings, which is up from the 2.5 to 3 percent default rate we've averaged since 2010.

Default rates provide an after-the-fact indication of problems with the economy. For those interested in determining the probability of problems ahead, there is another kernel of information that can be gleaned from the bond market that is a very good indicator of credit market stress: the pricing of credit default swaps (CDS). Comparable to hurricane insurance, a CDS offers protection for an investment if you hold the debt of a particular company, index, or country, and are concerned about the possibility of that borrower not being able to fulfill its obligations. The price of a credit default swap is determined by the risk associated with the probability of the underlying debt defaulting and some sophisticated math. For instance, hurricane insurance costs you a lot more when the black clouds can be seen approaching.

Credit default swaps became recognized in the last financial crisis as a tool for hedge funds to profit handsomely. However, they do serve an important role. CDSs are traded in basis points. A basis point is 1/100 of 1 percent. Therefore, if a CDS is trading at 200 basis points, the cost is 2 percent of the underlying (notional) bond value. To determine the probability of a default associated with a particular bond, all you have to do is look at the pricing in the CDS market. For instance, the Markit's iTraxx financial indices, which track the European financial groups' CDSs, serve as a proxy for credit risk in the sector. To date, they have jumped to new two-and-a-half-year highs. The subordinated debt index has jumped 110 basis points year-to-date to 191 basis points, while the senior debt index has climbed 52 basis points since the start of the year to 89 basis points.

It is not a foregone conclusion that a European financial bank default is imminent, considering in 2011 the credit default swap market reached similar levels and a default was averted. However, we must consider that, as the policies of Europe's various central banks have continually failed to jumpstart the European economy, it may only be a matter of time until a default becomes a reality.

FORTUNE TELLERS

A good friend of mine once told me that a million dollars' worth of (stock) tips will get you a million dollars' worth of losses. Truer words have never been spoken. We see them every day on television — market experts making predictions on where a stock will be trading in six months or a year. Or, even better, what levels major indices will be at by a certain date given x, y, and z.

Introducing to my right, in the Bull's corner at Dow 25,000, we have Thomas Lee, Mario Gabelli, Jeremy Siegel, Abby Joseph Cohen, and Jeff Saut. And to my left, in the Bear's corner at Dow 5,000, we have David Stockman, Peter Schiff, Marc Faber, Robert Prechter, and Harry Dent. Every one of these individuals happens to be very intelligent and at one time or another has made some extremely prescient market calls. However, if you were to grade their ability to correctly predict stocks or market direction consistently over the long term, I don't suspect any would receive a passing grade. More to my point, there is absolutely no one who can predict the future price of a stock or index with absolute certainty. But that does not mean nothing can be done to keep your losses small while letting your profits run.

Even a broken watch is correct twice a day. But of course a watch that is only right twice a day isn't much good. My same good friend said that too! So what's that piece of insight got to do with helping an investor keep his or her money safe without being able to predict the future? Let me explain. As I discussed in Chapter 2, there are numerous options for investors who want to protect the value of their portfolio. I have another pearl of wisdom — one that I have not shared with you yet — that I'd like to review.

Honesty. Do you have the courage to be completely honest with yourself? Because the difference between success and failure rests on your ability to be honest with yourself and to engage in clear, hard self-analysis. Do you and your financial advisor possess the skill to assess when you are wrong and take appropriate action quickly? I can't stress enough how important it is to have the mental capacity to admit when you're wrong. The results could be devastating if you don't. Understand that the stock market doesn't care who you are, when you plan to retire, or whose money is at stake. It can all be taken away very quickly. Don't let your own hubris get in the way of your future financial security.

Another indispensable quality is the ability to control your emotions. Saying this may be contradictory, considering dollar-cost averaging has been touted as a fail-safe method to achieve riches by the establishment for years. Dollar-cost averaging in this example refers to averaging down. Even though dollar-cost averaging can be a useful strategy when used properly, I have witnessed the destruction of many portfolios as investors continued to buy shares of stock that continued to drop in price to obscurity. Conversely, I've watched other investors sell stock short while rapidly climbing in price without reason, eventually draining their entire account with margin calls just as quickly. More recently, we've seen some very prominent hedge fund managers hang on to losing stocks that have contributed to their abysmal performance. No one is off limits when it comes to losing money. If a position is not working out, sometimes taking a loss is not only necessary, but essential in order to live another day. Of course, this is easier said than done!

Mark Spitznagel, the hedge fund co-manager of Universa and partner of Nassim Taleb, suggests that allocating a portion of your capital to portfolio insurance (put options) will ensure you are protected from any black swan event and allow you a greater concentration of equity exposure while doing so. It seems that Mark and I both agree that hedging portfolios using put options is most fitting.

The markets today seem very similar to the period of 1994 to 1995. At that time, there were a lot of issues causing the markets to slow, specifically the threat of rising interest rates, which made investors extremely uneasy. In 1994 the markets grinded sideways for the entire year when, without warning, in March 1995 the markets took off and had a terrific run right up until the Russian debacle in 1998. Since mid-May of 2015, the markets in North America have been flat to slightly negative. The bulls' rhetoric has been to declare that the best strategy for investors seeking to protect and increase the value of their portfolios is to increase exposure to European equities — a strategy that was most likely a response to the European central banks' efforts to preserve the European Union and NIRP. So much for that idea! Europe and Asia have fared the worst. To be fair, the bears have been decreeing the inevitable market collapse since 2011 to no avail either.

TABLE 7.7

Year-to-Date and 2015 ROI for Equities

	May 18, 2015– May 18, 2016	December 31, 2015
Equities	**1-Yr Return**	**YTD Return**
Dow Jones Industrial Average	−1.61%	1.74%
S&P 500	−1.69%	1.06%
NASDAQ 100	−5.39%	−4.80%
S&P/TSX Composite Index	−5.53%	7.51%
S&P/TSX 60	−5.17%	6.88%
Canadian Bonds		
Government Short Bonds	−0.94%	−0.25%
Government Long Bonds	2.41%	2.49%
Government Bond Universe	0.82%	0.70%
Cash	1% annually	
European Markets		
Britain FTSE 100	−9.39%	−0.51%
Germany DAX	−17.06%	−8.49%
France CAC40	−13.34%	−5.77%
Italy MIB	−24.41%	−17.13%
Greece	−25.36%	−0.43%
Spain IBEX35	−21.21%	−6.86%
Asian Markets		
Shanghai	−35.43%	−20.60%
Hong Kong (Hang Seng)	−26.09%	−9.13%
Japan Nikkei 225	−15.35%	−11.80%

For investors who were chasing returns, the assumption that being invested in global equities over the 2015–2016 period would have produced tidy profits has resulted in considerable disappointment. In North America, certainly, holding cash or bonds in your portfolio instead of equities would have served you considerably better. What will happen, moving forward, is anyone's guess, but as you have already heard me say many times over, I believe caution is warranted.

As discussed, no one is able to forecast future market direction with any accuracy. However, this does not mean that you should not engage in the timely monitoring of new information, and take immediate action based on that data. For example, if you are fully invested in risk assets (equities) and monitor market conditions daily, you may have the availability to make timely decisions. That being said, though, in all my years of experience, I have known very few who have had both the time and emotional fortitude to engage with the market in that kind of intimate way. Markets move at incredible speeds today, and their level of volatility is extraordinary, likely because of high-frequency trading, making this strategy hard to execute and a very risky proposition. As a result, I would not advise any non-professional investor to attempt to go this route.

ADVANCED STRATEGIES

I cannot stress enough that buying stocks at the right time is the most important strategy in order to become a winner at the investment table. Simply put: buy low and sell high. But let's assume you've made all this money, are waiting around for next bull market, and are anxious. How do you manage this feeling? A number of investment tools in the market today can be used to protect your pile of dough. I want to teach you how to use these instruments for their intended purpose — keeping you out of trouble. Remember, making money is one thing. Keeping it is another.

The topics I will be covering in this section are complex option strategies, and for those who are not well versed in options, you may find it difficult to follow along. If that's the case, I would suggest that you do a bit of homework on basic option strategies (see Recommended Reading for some sources) and then come back to re-visit this section when you're more comfortable with the subject. Okay, here we go.

DELTA

The fundamental tenet of option pricing is delta, which is represented by the Greek letter Δ. It refers to the change in the price of an option relative to a change in the price of the underlying interest, such as a common share. Generally speaking, the delta of an at-the-money option is 0.5. That is, if the share price moves in either direction $1, the option price will gain or lose $0.50. The more an option is in the money, the greater the delta. It makes sense that, for an option that is deep in the money, as the share price changes, the option price will change almost equally. Conversely, a deep out-of-the-money option price will change only marginally, if at all, if there is a change in the price of the shares.

The basic equation for understanding option structure and pricing is referred to as put–call parity. As you will soon observe, rearranging the equation will help you understand many different option positions and strategies.

Strike Price = Stock + Put – Call

Looking up an Apple quote when the stock is trading at $92.70, I find that the offer on the three-month 92.50 put is $5.35 and the bid on the three-month 92.50 call is $5.25. The put offer is used because the position is long (buying), and the call bid is used because the position is short (selling). Note the put–call parity equation also indicates a long put (+) and short call (−).

92.5 = $92.70 + $5.35 – $5.25

The equation does not quite equal because the cost of borrowing capital and any applicable dividends have been intentionally left out for simplicity.

Now, with the equation established, it can be rearranged to produce many different positions or equivalents. I'm also changing the nomenclature for easier understanding.

- Synthetic Long Stock = Long Call + Short Put
- Synthetic Short Stock = Long Put + Short Call
- Long Stock + Long Put + Short Call = Long Collar
- Short Stock + Long Call + Short Put = Short Collar

- Long Stock + Short Call = Covered Call
- Long Stock + Short Call = Short Put
- Covered Call = Short Put

A synthetic short should be added to your tool box for when you want to short a stock and there is none available to borrow in inventory. There may be additional collateral (margin) required compared to outright shorting stock, but it would be based on your broker's own internal risk controls, even though they are identical trades.

In another situation, if you are holding a stock and the position is declining, you may want to protect your downside by adding a synthetic short to the position until conditions reverse. Notice that by adding a long put and short call to a long stock position, you establish a position known as a long collar. Just a word of caution: if you create a short position using options with the same strikes against a long stock position, the transaction may be refused because of a rule known as "shorting the box." Basically, the trade is interpreted as tax avoidance by Revenue Canada. To avoid this scenario, you can separate the strikes to create the collar.

A long collar is a position I discussed in Chapter 2. It allows investors to have their cake and eat it too — that is, to have a small amount of upside capital appreciation and collect a juicy dividend, all the while assuming very little to no risk. When interest rates were higher than at their current levels, a slightly out-of-the-money call sale would have completely funded an at-the-money put purchase. However, today a long at-the-money put is more expensive than an out-of-the-money call. This condition leaves a collar strategist with limited choices — either buy a put further out of the money or fund the put with a debit put spread, thereby defeating the whole purpose of downside protection in the event of a sharp price decline.

It is common thinking in the investment community that writing a call against a long stock position is a very conservative strategy. However, ask someone to write a naked put and they'll think you've lost your mind. I'm always amused by the reaction of an investor when they realize these strategies share the same principle. Writing puts is a strategy that is only to be used for dollar-cost averaging or buying additional shares below market value. A put seller should not write more puts than stock they are prepared to own. Furthermore, in an extremely bullish market, do not write puts hoping to accumulate stock on pullbacks. Nothing is more frustrating than writing puts and watching a stock advance ten, twenty, thirty, or more points. Even more important, reduce or suspend all put writing in a bear market.

In the late 1990s, during the technology boom, many companies resorted to buying back their own shares to boost earnings. More cleverly, a select few savvy CEOs were writing puts to commit to buying back their companies' shares rather than outright buybacks. As a consequence, the premiums they collected became so profitable that earnings were improved, in turn causing their own share prices to advance higher without spending any cash at all.

Because covered call writing is such a common strategy, I'm going to go through a few scenarios of what can go wrong and what to do about it when it does. The first and most obvious problem results from a stock falling in price. The natural tendency when that happens is to wait for the short call to expire before taking any action. All this usually does, however, is give the stock more time to decline further. Your mental stop depends on your trailing stop (pain threshold); if you reach that pain threshold, you should sell the stock and buy back the call. It is always better to take a small loss than wait to take a larger one.

The second problem occurs when a stock modestly advances above the short call strike price, or when it becomes in the money. The good news is that, if your outlook on the stock changes and you believe it may rally higher, you do not necessarily have to give up your stock to the call exercise. You may be able to "roll" the call for little to no cost. The call roll will be further out in time premium and higher in strike price, thereby allowing you to capture further gains from the stock appreciation. Basically, you are funding the existing call repurchase from the proceeds of the longer-dated, higher strike call being sold.

For example, in early May 2016 Disney common stock was trading at $102. Let's assume you wrote the May 100 call previously and you really didn't want to give up the stock. The May 100 calls were being offered at $2.30. You looked at an option chain and saw that the October 105 calls were bid at $3.30. You decided to buy back the May call, sell the October call, and collect a $1 credit. You effectively accomplished three things: you lowered your cost per share by another $1, allowed for an additional $5 of share appreciation, and were able to continue to collect any dividends paid between May and October.

The third problem arises when a stock shoots through the short call strike and advances deep into the money. The first option is to let the stock go and move on. The second option is to buy back the deep in-the-money short call. One way this can be funded is out of pocket, which I don't recommend. The other is by selling a portion of the long stock position to cover the cost so that the remaining unencumbered shares have further potential to run higher.

Finally, I want to discuss a hot topic that every stock investor has had to face at one time or another. Everyone has had an experience of buying a stock after doing their research and, as soon as it is bought, it immediately begins to drop in price. At this point you have a few options: sell, hold, or average down. If you sell, you lock in a capital loss. If you hold, chances are good in favourable market conditions that the stock will recover. If you average down, you've effectively lowered your average cost per share but have committed more capital to an unprofitable trade, a double-edged sword. "Buying the dip" in a bull market usually will result in a favourable outcome. However, there will eventually come a time when averaging down could lead to devastation.

Here is a solution that effectively produces similar results to averaging down, with one enormous difference — it requires no additional out-of-pocket expense. It is called the "stock repair." As far as I'm concerned you can use it to be greedy, too. Referring back to Disney, let's say you purchased 100 shares of Disney in December 2015 for $110. In May 2016, Disney was trading at $106 and, based on current market conditions, you would sell if you got back to break-even. Unfortunately, Disney's earnings came in below estimates in May and the shares fell back down to $102. Now what do you do?

Well, what if I told you that you could get out of Disney with all your money if it only recovered back to $105, with no further out-of-pocket expense. Would you be interested? I thought so. Here's how it works. Again, the option chain shows the October 100 calls are offered at $6.20. The October 105 calls are bid at $3.30. You own 100 shares of Disney, so you buy one October 100 call for $6.20 and sell two October 105 calls for $3.30 and collect a credit of $0.40. If Disney shares are at $105 or better in

October 2016, you collect $10,500 for your shares and make $500 on the bull call spread, breaking even. As a bonus, you also collect an additional $0.40 and still receive any dividends paid.

> Disney at $102
> Buy 1 October 100 call @ $6.20
> Sell 2 October 105 calls @ $3.30

VEGA

The second fundamental tenet of option pricing is volatility, or vega, which is represented by the Greek letter K, or kappa. Besides delta, the second-largest contributor to an options price change is volatility. Volatility must be understood properly because it has the potential to turn a winning trade into an unprofitable one and a losing trade into a complete washout. Event trades, such as earnings announcements or Food and Drug Administration decisions, are good examples of volatility aberrations. Typically, volatility is much higher before an event because of uncertainty. This in turn inflates option prices. Let me provide you with a hypothetical scenario.

A drug company is expecting an announcement for the approval of a new drug treatment. The stock is trading at $110 and the at-the-money call and put are both $6. These prices indicate an implied volatility of 93 percent. Two investors with opposing views each buy a $115 call for $4 and a $105 put for $3.70. After the market closes, the announcement is made and the drug is given approval. The stock opens the following day at $118, up $8, or 7 percent. However, the volatility drops to 40 percent. As a result, the call's new price is $4.40 and the put is worthless. For the call buyer, the stock price moved $8 and the call price appreciated by a measly $0.40, or 10 percent. The put, on the other hand, was a complete washout, making both trades inappropriate given the circumstances.

Option strategists may sometimes mention the implied move for a stock with a known event anticipated in the near future. The implied move can be estimated by adding the two nearest at-the-money call and put prices and dividing by the stock price. For the above example, the implied move in price is equal to 10.9 percent. However, the price move in my example was only 7 percent.

$$\frac{\$6 + \$6}{\$110} = 10.9 \text{ percent}$$

It is imperative that, when using any option strategy for a purpose other than hedging, you adapt your strategy to the current market conditions. Generally speaking, this means that for most of a market cycle your bias should be bullish. Therefore, your strategies should reflect a bullish viewpoint. For a small portion of time that the market is in a correction phase, your bias should be bearish and your strategies reflect a bearish outlook. In my opinion, this is where most investors make their biggest mistakes: failing to adapt their investment ideas to changing market conditions.

8

HOW DO YOU KNOW WHEN THE MARKET HAS REACHED THE TOP?

Signs of a market top are beginning to appear. Merger activity is heating up, as it did during the technology bubble prior to the year 2000. We have recently witnessed the announcements of some very large mergers, including the proposed $85 billion AT&T deal with Time Warner and Qualcomm's $45 billion bid for NXP Semiconductors. It just so happens that 2015 was a record year for mergers and acquisitions — the value of global deals topped $4.6 trillion. More telling is the performance of specific industry sectors that historically tend to outperform in the late stages of a market cycle. Those sectors include technology, industrials, and materials, which are incidentally three of the best-performing market sectors in 2016.

As stock markets reach new highs, many individual stocks do not, which makes pinpointing the top of the market very difficult. For example, looking at the current internals of the S&P 500 warrants considerable pause. Only twenty-eight stocks in the S&P 500 (less than 6 percent of the index) are at new highs, yet the market index itself is making all-time highs. What could account for this unusual paradox? Light trading volumes and rotating leadership? Unfortunately, individual stocks reach new highs at different times, causing confusion for investors looking for the market top. This may be why investors fail to act until it is too late. However, the opposite is also true: stocks almost always reach the bottom of a market cycle at the same time, making a market bottom much easier to identify than a top.

We know that institutional money managers are considerably nervous about the current market environment. Their two biggest concerns are geopolitical risk and protectionism. In response, portfolio cash allocations are close to peak levels and portfolio insurance is being purchased extensively. Which raises the question: Who is buying stocks? The companies themselves, of course, through massive stock buyback programs. Cheap money has enabled companies to financially engineer earnings expectations by simply reducing their number of shares outstanding. Recall the formula for earnings per share is as follows:

$$\text{Earnings per Share} = \frac{\text{Net Earnings}}{\text{Common Outstanding}}$$

Reduce the number of common outstanding and presto, earnings per share increases. Which leads to my next question: How long can companies continue to increase their debt load to sustain earnings? Or, even better: What happens when interest rates are normalized?

Central bankers have also played a role. We know that asset purchases, including sovereign debt and investment- and non-investment-grade bonds, have been made by the Bank of Japan and the European Central Bank since 2011. Now they are buying assets on stock exchanges around the globe as well. More to the point, they're monetizing assets, meaning central banks are simply printing money and using it to purchase assets with economic value. The real purpose of this action is to prop up markets in the face of panic sell-offs, such as Britain's departure from the European Union. Does this seem responsible or even logical? Recently I overheard a money manager describing the situation as comparable to shuffling chairs on the deck of the Titanic. It is inevitable that the ship is going to go down — it's just a matter of time!

RESPECT THE OPINION OF A FEW

In 2006 I was on a road trip to New York for a weekend with friends. Someone had brought with them a Merrill Lynch report. We chatted about it, noting that it outlined some troubling concerns about the state of the U.S. housing market, concerns that were backed up with some interesting facts. Ironically, not more than a few years later, Merrill Lynch would collapse as a result of the collateral damage of the housing crisis.

The author of the prescient report was David Rosenberg, who returned to Canada after the housing crisis and is now employed as chief economist with Gluskin Sheff. From time to time he makes an appearance on BNN or is interviewed in a newspaper and discusses his thoughts on the economy and related topics. When David has an opinion, it is usually a good idea to pay attention.

Besides David Rosenberg, there is a select group of very smart stock market experts who I pay close attention to. Considering no one has a monopoly on ideas, gathering intelligence from a few respected sources is always helpful. I have found the opinions of the following individuals on current market conditions and ongoing events to be honest, insightful, and well-timed.

Jim Rogers's career seems relatively short in retrospect, considering he's been retired and managing his own money for almost forty years. He is best known for co-managing the Quantum Hedge fund in the 1970s with George Soros, where in ten years they realized a return of 4,900 percent. He wrote a book called *The Investment Biker* that describes his adventures travelling the world on his BMW motorcycle, investigating potential investment opportunities.

In an interview in *Barron's* on November 16, 2015, Jim expressed his concerns about the global markets today and advocated extreme caution. His view on the world is that we have been in a bull market for six and a half years, and with all the money-printing and debt that has been built up over those years, this market cycle will undoubtedly end badly. Even more interesting is his take on the catalyst: "When you take a look at previous bear markets, they usually start with a small, marginal country that has trouble that snowballs, and the next thing you know, we're all in trouble." In my opinion, his advice to proceed carefully at this point in the market cycle should not be taken lightly. This is good advice from one of the best.

The Oracle of Omaha is someone who has stood the test of time. Warren Buffett is the authority on value investing. There have been many books co-authored on his philosophy and stock selection process, but I prefer some of Buffett's classic quotes. Three of my favourites are "You don't know who's swimming naked until the tide goes out"; "The weapons of mass destruction that scare me the most are financial"; and "Be fearful when others are greedy and greedy when others are fearful." The first refers to corporate corruption that is exposed when market volatility increases; the second refers to derivatives; and the third is another way of saying buy low and sell high. Unless you own Berkshire Hathaway shares and attend the company's annual meetings, you may not have an opportunity to hear from Buffett often. The internet is a good resource for finding what he's been commenting on recently.

A chief investment strategist who is equally as talented as David Rosenberg is James W. Paulsen of Wells Capital Management. The "Economic and Market Perspective" he pens is filled with insightful and thought-provoking commentary on existing market conditions and is supported by current data and historical comparisons. His reports are sometimes technical but are filled with lots of supporting graphs for those who are more visual, like me. Keeping in mind that his opinions might be softened for the sake of his readership, his market calls are as close to the truth as one may find. His reports can be found at www.wellscap.com.

As well as following the advice of these investors and analysts, anyone who is serious about staying well-informed on global markets must subscribe to the *Economist*. Staying current on financial markets requires weekly review and a worldly perspective, and no other publication does a better job of that. The following list of *Economist* issues requires no other explanation of their significance other than their dates.

•	January 9, 1999	How to Make Mergers Work
•	January 30, 1999	Why Internet Shares Will Fall to Earth When the Bubble Bursts
•	January 20, 2007	Rich Man, Poor Man: The Winners and Losers of Globalisation
•	March 24, 2007	The Trouble with the Housing Market
•	August 18, 2007	Surviving the Markets
•	November 17, 2007	America's Vulnerable Economy: Recession in America
•	June 13, 2015	Watch Out: The World Is Not Ready for the Next Recession

- November 14, 2015   The Chronicles of Debt: A Saga That Haunts the World Economy
- February 20, 2016   The World Economy: Out of Ammo?
- May 7, 2016   Inside: A Special Report on China's Coming Debt Bust

Despite the good advice that can be gleaned from all of these sources, remember that no one, and I mean no one, will take better care of your money than you. That being said, many studies have proven that people who use a financial advisor do better over time than those who do not.

According to the Econometric study conducted by Claude Montmarquette in 2012, investors who have a financial advisor for four to six years have more than 1.5 times the assets of those with no advice. Between seven and fourteen years, the amount of assets almost doubles. For fifteen years or more, the amount is 2.73 times greater. More importantly, the impact of advice arises from factors other than stock picking. A greater amount of assets is attributed to increased rates of savings, better portfolio diversification, and greater tax efficiency. Best of all, having a financial advisor increases a person's level of confidence that they will have enough money to retire comfortably.

The challenge for those seeking financial advice is to find an advisor you like. Fortunately, in Canada, because of the oversight of our regulators, your money is equally safe with all firms, regardless of their size. This is owing to their three-sided organizational structure. Generally speaking, recommendations are made to retail clients by a qualified professional. A portfolio manager selects the individual securities, and a separate trust company holds the assets.

In almost all cases, investors get into trouble when they are solicited by sources outside of this type of structure — by parties who hold your assets as well as manage the investments. In such cases, the first question you should ask yourself when being solicited is, "What agenda does this person have?" This is good advice for any business transaction you may be involved in, period.

David Rosenberg was quite confident about the markets up until a short time ago. Recently he has begun to express concern over employment and GDP growth in the United States. Now that David has turned decidedly bearish, I would take heed. As already mentioned, Jim Rogers believes a major market correction is imminent. Warren Buffett and Jim Paulsen tend not to make market directional calls but will usually comment on specific occurrences. To date, the *Economist* has not called the end of the seven-year bull market but has made reference many times to the dismal state of Europe and Japan and the mounting debt of governments worldwide. We need only ask what will be the catalyst or tipping point to shift the direction the other way.

PAY ATTENTION TO THE HEADLINES

When you're looking for investment ideas, the business section of the newspaper is as good a place to look as any. When you're looking for investment advice, speak to a financial advisor. What sets these two entities apart is specific knowledge of you and your investment needs. A newspaper writes about the economy in general or about specific industries or companies, and its writers may make recommendations based on their analyses. However, these recommendations are general — not aimed at any particular investor. A financial advisor knows you and your unique circumstances.

I have discussed a number of sources of economic and market indicators throughout the book, but I believe it's crucial that you understand the limits of the media. It is not my intention to question the reputation or character of the business media. I approach the topic with an open mind. However, experience shows that the investment ideas discussed in print, other than the few that I've mentioned, make better contrary indicators than sources of actual recommendations. The reason is twofold. Although the media have a moral and an ethical responsibility to act in the best interest of their audience, they are not accountable to them. If I recommend a stock to a client and it declines in value, it is real money they've lost if the stock is sold. No one can be right all of the time, but I'd better be more right than wrong or I will lose my client. Secondly, media personalities are human beings who have emotions and get caught up in the hype of market mania just as easily as the general public.

Case in point: Valeant Pharmaceutical was, until recently, *the* sought-after Canadian company to own. However, the incredible performance of Valeant alone would not have made it an appropriate investment for many investors. Why? The risk associated with owning it. Still, on July 24, 2015, a Canadian national newspaper published an article titled "Why There's No Bubble in Biotech." The piece provided information about the health care sector and focused on the success of Valeant's acquisition business strategy. Valeant was trading on that day for $326. Four months later Valeant was trading for $95, 70 percent lower. Chasing a hot stock that has already advanced to nosebleed territory is not recommended. This is a perfect example of what not to do. The guiding principle of this book is to buy low and sell high, not the opposite.

The following quotes are from a number of newspaper articles written over the last seventeen years that undeniably demonstrate that history does repeat itself and we are likely close to the next market correction. I have purposely mixed up their publication dates to reinforce my thesis. For fun, try to guess the dates published before looking at the answers, which come after the list.

1. "Coming into [date] there was great debate whether this enthusiasm could continue, but based on our data, there seems to be no signs of slowing down."
2. "Wall Street bonuses set new records."
3. "Private equity rules as buyout kings ... Nothing is beyond the reach of private equity — nothing."
4. "Stocks soar on merger speculation ... a flurry of merger proposals inspired a frenzy of takeover speculation yesterday that helped drive U.S. stock markets to record highs and took Canadian exchanges along for the ride."
5. "The heavy demand, as much as 20 times more than the intended offering size, allowed many issuers to sell their new shares at higher prices and better valuations."
6. "A liquidity boom has pushed financial assets to heights worldwide and driven investors into riskier corners of the market in search of better returns ... Central banks and the monetary policies they adopt play a big part in flooding markets with money."
7. "A confluence of factors are likely driving this activity, such as companies' rising stock prices, low interest rates and private equity and pension funds flush with piles of cash to invest."

8. "Hong Kong bank branches have resembled movie theatres on opening night, with lineups queuing out the door as hopeful investors jockey to buy shares."

9. "Initial public offerings in the United States have already reached a record value this year, with the rest of November and December still to go."

10. "The size of this week's deals underscores the confidence that chief executive officers have in the stock market after the Dow Jones industrial average rose to another record on Nov. 8, and the S&P 500 approaches a six-year high. Private equity firms also are taking advantage of buoyant stock indexes to raise money from public investors."

And last but not least ...

11. "Use those pullbacks as buying opportunities because basically the fundamentals for North America and global stock markets are still quite positive ... I don't think there's any reason to panic."

1. *National Post*, July 25, 2015
2. *Globe and Mail*, January 12, 2006
3. *Globe and Mail*, January 2, 2007
4. *Globe and Mail*, January 7, 1999
5. *Globe and Mail*, August 17, 2015
6. *Globe and Mail*, January 2, 2007
7. *Globe and Mail*, July 2, 2015
8. *Globe and Mail*, September 30, 2006
9. *Globe and Mail*, November 4, 1999
10. *Globe and Mail*, November 14, 2006
11. *Globe and Mail*, April 5, 2007

You'll notice the most bullish quotes were printed before the most stunning corrections and that the most recent quotes are similar in tone to those.

INVESTOR PSYCHOLOGY

I want to ask you a serious question. What causes an individual equity to appreciate in value? I'm not being facetious. Before reading ahead, think for a moment and try to answer this question honestly. If you answered the question the way I assume most would, you probably said something to the effect that a company will appreciate in value if it is consistently growing revenue and profits. Another reason you might give for a company's shares increasing in value is that it has a unique product or service that gives it a distinct advantage over the competition or has high barriers of entry to limit competition, like a monopoly.

Well, if you chose any of the above answers, you would be incorrect. The reason an individual equity goes up in price is that it has buyers who are interested in buying that company's stock. What causes it to go up dramatically is large buyers. This is better known as institutional sponsorship. The key to making big money in the stock market is being able to identify the equities into which big money is flowing.

How do you identify these equities? First, we can start by eliminating equities that are not likely to receive big money flow. Institutional investors have restrictions placed on them that make certain investments ineligible. Restrictions may include equities that trade below $3 to $5 or have small floats (the number of shares traded publicly), small market capitalization, minimum holding requirements, illiquidity, or concentration in portfolios. Therefore, investors should select only equities that trade on the S&P TSX 60, S&P 500, or NASDAQ 100, since their constituents are more likely to attract big money flows.

I have had this discussion with investors for many years. Contrary to popular belief, it is just as easy for a stock trading at $100 to double as it is for a $0.10 stock. An equity bought at the beginning of the next bull market that attracts institutional sponsorship has the ability to appreciate a lot — indeed, it will likely more than double in value.

How do you identify institutional ownership of an individual equity? For U.S. and Canadian inter-listed companies, I have found Nasdaq.com very helpful. The left column from the Quotes dropdown menu, under Holdings, lists the holdings of all institutional ownership. For Canadian companies, the one source I know, which, admittedly, has only limited information, is Morningstar, a subscription-based website. Sedar.com is the Canadian website for public company filings, but it is hard to navigate. Keep in mind that institutional sponsorship is just another gauge to add to your tool box of indicators.

One aspect of institutional ownership that should be remembered is that, while it can help to drive up the price of a company's shares, it can also work the other way. For instance, if a company has a large institutional ownership weighting and experiences a damaging report or material change, its stock price can be driven lower very quickly as large blocks of shares are dumped. A recent example of this is Valeant Pharmaceuticals. When it was finally discovered that its roll-up strategy would only work until people could no longer afford its enormously inflated drug prices, all bets were off.

On May 1, 2000, a monumental event occurred that affected 500,000 Canadian shareholders. Its aftershocks are still felt today. On that day, Bell Canada spun off Nortel Networks. It was the final days of the technology boom, and the North American stock markets were staging the biggest advance in history. At its peak, Nortel represented over 30 percent of the value of the TSE 300 index and had a market capitalization of C$398 billion. Prior to the spin-off, Bell Canada was one of the companies most widely held by retail and institutional investors in Canada. It had a history of being a safe blue chip company that consistently delivered solid earnings and dividend growth. It was also a well-understood business. Many retail investors held BCE as a core position in their portfolios, so it wasn't uncommon to find accounts with two thousand shares or more. As a result of the Nortel spin-off, the adjusted cost base of BCE and the newly acquired Nortel shares dropped considerably. However, the increase to investors' portfolio values after the Nortel spin-off was nearly 40 percent.

- 2,000 shares of BCE prior to Nortel spin-off was worth approximately $350,000
- 2,000 shares of BCE plus 3,140 new shares of Nortel was worth approximately $500,000

There were a number of reasons why very few shareholders could be persuaded to reduce their holdings. Among the major ones were the significant capital gains tax that would be triggered if they sold and the hubris that permeated investors' psyches during that period. As attractive as the growth in investor portfolio value caused by the Nortel spin-off was, its rise did not equal the growth of other investments held in portfolios during this time; in fact, to the best of my recollection, many others doubled in value.

Unfortunately, very few investors parted with their beloved shares. In September of 2000, Nortel traded at the high of $124, but by August of 2002 a Nortel share was worth $0.47.

The aftermath of the Nortel disaster reaches far beyond the losses experienced by its shareholders. The Nortel employees' pension plan held Nortel shares, so many have no pension to speak of today.

Events like these seem to repeat themselves over and over. For instance, the automobile industry suffered a similar fate in the 2008–2009 market correction when shares fell precipitously, government bail-outs followed, and pension assets were lost. The technology boom produced similar momentous losses when it ended too. I will never forget a conversation I had with a client during the hysteria of the boom. It went something like this:

> Client: Hi, Alan, I want you to buy a stock.
> Alan: Okay, what's the name of the stock?
> Client: [insert any dot.com name here]
> Alan: What do they do?
> Client: Not sure.
> Alan: Are they making money?
> Client: I don't think so.
> Alan: What's the price of the stock?
> Client: [insert any value here]
> Alan: What price do you want me to place the order at?
> Client: Market.
> Alan: Really?
> Client: Yes, I want to make sure we buy it.
> Alan: What is your target price?
> Client: Don't have one.

As you can see, irrational exuberance — emotions — causes investors to lose rational thought. In 2007, the U.S. real estate market created equally irrational behaviour that is not unlike the price appreciation Canadian real estate is experiencing today.

There are a number of take-aways from studying investor behaviour. First, never make decisions that are influenced by your emotions. That's easier said than done, I know, but I keep repeating this throughout the book because I believe it is the most important rule to follow. Fear and greed are our enemies.

Second, never make investment decisions based on tax considerations. Investments and taxes share a common thread, but the thread is easily broken. Invariably, after Nortel became worthless, the chorus of investors all sang the same song: "Should have paid the tax!" That applies to both buying investments as well as selling. Related to this is another blunder that comes to mind: labour-sponsored funds. Many investors bought LSVCCs (labour-sponsored venture capital corporations) for the same reason: tax savings. As time passed, most labour-sponsored funds' values vanished through a series of risky investments and poor investment management. Therefore, rule number two is to keep tax considerations out of the decision-making process.

The third rule is that you must always diversify. If your employment income is derived from the same company that oversees your pension assets, then you are what is known in the industry as over-concentrated. In other words, if the company that writes your paycheque also has your pension assets invested in its own shares, quickly extricate yourself. Simply put, you have too many eggs in one basket.

MARGIN DEBT (LEVERAGE)

If the market is the engine, consider margin debt the fuel. What is margin? Margin is a term used to describe the capital an investor puts up of their own money. With your capital deposited into a margin account, a brokerage firm will lend you cash (margin debt) in addition to your own for added purchasing power, at a nominal interest rate, of course.

Currently, the margin lending rate at most brokerages varies between 4 and 5 percent. Depending on security selection and other risk factors, margin rates may increase or decrease. For consistency, I will use a 50 percent margin rate, considering most equities qualify. As you will observe, leverage can be very rewarding but also very devastating. The reason a margin account is used more pervasively than other sources of borrowed money is ease of access — no application, no income verification, no qualifying.

At a 50 percent margin rate, an investor can double his or her initial investment. In other words, if an investor has $100,000 of capital, a brokerage will lend you an additional $100,000 for a total investable amount of $200,000. Now, referring to my earlier comments on leveraging, you can easily see how it is possible to lose not only your own money, but much more — in fact, in the following example, $100,000 more!

TABLE 8.1

Shares	4,000 shares at $50	Loan at 50%	$100,000
purchased at $50	= $200,000	Original margin	$100,000
		Margin required	$0
Shares drop	4,000 shares at $40	Loan at 50%	$80,000
to $40	= $160,000	Original margin	$100,000
		Margin required	$20,000
Shares drop	4,000 shares at $10	Loan at 50%	$20,000
to $10	= $40,000	Original margin	$100,000
		Margin required	$80,000
Shares drop	4,000 shares at $0	Loan at 50%	$0
to $0	= $0	Original margin	$100,000
		Margin required	$100,000

This scenario would not take place in the real world because if our investor did not provide the margin required at $40, a portion of the shares would be sold by the brokerage to cover the deficit. If the shares continued to fall further, more shares would be sold until either the margin was covered or the account was liquidated. Another way to calculate the margin required at a 50 percent margin rate is to appreciate that $0.50 is required for every $1 loss per share. In other words, from the initial $50 purchase to $40, the loss is $10 per share. Therefore, $0.50 × $10 × 4,000 shares equals $20,000. I have purposely not provided a scenario for the potential upside to leverage because the downside is all that matters. The upside will take care of itself.

Despite the potential risks of using margin debt, the last six years of artificially low rates have made cheap money too enticing to resist and have given investors the debt fuel to propel markets higher. The correlation of margin debt to index levels in the last twenty-five years is an impressive 94.8 percent for the NYSE and 91.9 percent for the TSX.

FIGURE 8.1
Correlation of Margin Debt to Index Levels of NYSE

Source: NYSEdata.com (margin debt) and Yahoo! Finance (S&P 500)

FIGURE 8.2
Correlation of Margin Debt to Index Levels of TSX

Source: IIROC (margin debt) and Yahoo! Finance (S&P TSX)

New money is what drives the stock market higher, and many feel that if investors are making money, there is no problem with investing more. No doubt this is what feels comfortable, but it does not necessarily make leveraging appropriate. In fact, nothing could be further from the truth. As the markets reach new all-time highs, the right strategy is to pare back gains and build a larger cash position. Adding to new or existing equity positions with borrowed money in the later stage of a bull market is quite simply reckless behaviour.

The simple fact is that margin is the fuel for market corrections as well. Recently, the U.S. equity markets have started to climb back toward their all-time highs. As well, margin debit balances are also climbing back to all-time highs. If a correction occurs, as is likely, one can see from Table 8.1 that, as markets fall and shares decline, margin is required to replenish accounts. If the markets stabilize, margin requirements ease and all is resumed. If markets encounter a more protracted correction, shares are sold into a falling market, these sales drive share prices lower, more shares are sold, and something more ominous potentially unfolds.

This is essentially what was responsible for the market crash of October 19, 1987, known as Black Monday. Portfolio managers shorted index futures to cushion the loss to their equity portfolios as the markets began to drop. This caused index futures to trade at a substantial discount to the cash (equity) market. Arbitrageurs then bought index futures (being sold by portfolio managers) and shorted the cash market (equities portfolio managers were trying to hedge) to capture the risk-free price discrepancy, thus intensifying the market decline.

In summary, it should be understood that no one indicator outlined in this chapter can accurately predict the top of a market conclusively. These are just pieces of the puzzle that, when placed together, can create an accurate picture on which to base our decisions. Examining the graphs in Figures 8.1 and 8.2, we can conclude that margin debt today has surpassed levels reached in 2007. Additionally, margin debt is at best a coincidental indicator at a market top. One irrefutable fact that margin debt does provide us with is that, just as it adds additional fuel to a rising market, it exacerbates the plunge as well. However, it does so at an exponentially faster rate.

STOCK BUYBACKS

The practice of companies using their cash to repurchase their own stock is not necessarily a sign of trouble, but it may be an indication that the longer term could be problematic once the buying eventually ends. To understand what the underlying implications are, let's look at how to calculate earnings per share:

$$\text{Earnings per Share} = \frac{\text{Net Earnings}}{\text{Common Outstanding}}$$

When a company buys its shares back, the number of shares outstanding is reduced, resulting in higher earnings per share. On the surface, this may seem fine, but what is the motivation? Corporations have many things they can do with cash, including pay a dividend, buy back stock, pay down debt, make an acquisition, or reinvest (research and development). If a company can earn a higher return than its cost of capital, it should acquire or reinvest. If it can't, it should return it to shareholders.

If the rationale for a share buyback is to allow the CEO, who will have earnings-per-share targets, to reward him- or herself, this may be counter-productive. Shareholders usually welcome buybacks, believing they lift share prices, and they usually do in the short term. In the long term, however, the benefits of repurchase programs are open to question because the timing of buybacks is entirely at management's discretion, and there is a tendency for management teams to initiate a buy at market highs rather than lows. This is because in the late stages of a market cycle, earnings growth begins to slow. In order to counteract this, earnings can be propped up temporarily by reducing the number of shares outstanding.

Companies will often buy shares to offset the impact of the exercise of employee stock options, and depending on the number of options outstanding, the buyback may be used to manipulate the share price and prevent it from dropping. Share buybacks have also been known to help management dress up, or financially engineer, ratios involving per-share calculations by which quarterly performance is measured. Have buybacks become a necessity because corporate revenue and organic earnings growth have been slowing for several months? The evidence does seem to suggest this is the case.

Figuring out the long-term impact of repurchases on share prices can be difficult. The pros and cons of individual company buybacks are often explored on sites like Seeking Alpha (www.seekingalpha.com) and The Motley Fool (www.fool.com). Low interest rates have undoubtedly fuelled the current buyback frenzy. Interest rates being as low as they are, it makes more sense for companies to finance a reasonable portion of their balance sheets with debt rather than equity. However, over the longer term, insufficient capital spending means less GDP growth, fewer jobs, and downward pressure on wages.

Dividend distributions are a different matter. They, too, make no contribution to the growth of a company, but at least they put spare cash into the pockets of shareholders and not management. Dividends reward long-term shareholders, while buybacks fatten the pockets of executives and reward short-term investors. Where there is a lot of buyback activity, there is usually a hedge fund. Hedge funds typically have only their own self-interests in mind when owning companies shares. However, lately even activists have significantly reduced their campaigns for shareholder distributions. This may be a sign the companies are being more stingy with their cash or that a lot of companies may have hit a wall in terms of organic growth in the new world paradigm.

It should not come as a surprise that the greatest amount of total dollars spent in stock buybacks coincides with market tops. The dividend yield of the S&P 500 has been consistently hovering around 2 percent. As I have already suggested, I believe that market indices have been held up by massive stock buyback programs for some time now. According to the Factset Buyback Quarterly dated September 20, 2016, there has been a considerable drop in buyback spending in the second half of 2016. The last time we witnessed a similar decline was in the first quarter of 2008. Furthermore, some 137 companies in the S&P 500 have spent more money on buybacks than they generated in earnings. Is this the beginning of something more ominous? We will know soon enough.

INITIAL PUBLIC OFFERINGS

History doesn't repeat itself 100 percent of the time, but sometimes it will rhyme. Do the size and volume of initial public offerings (IPOs) correlate with the top of a market cycle? It is my contention that in the past such stock market happenings have signalled the end of previous bull markets. An increase in the value of IPOs is telling us that a correction may be approaching once again. I cannot prove causality, but there can be no dispute that a strong correlation does exist.

Prior to 2009, the United States was the leading issuer of IPOs in terms of total value. It passed the baton, however, and China became the leading issuer, raising $73 billion (almost double the amount of money raised on the New York Stock Exchange and the NASDAQ combined) up to the end of November 2011. The Hong Kong Stock Exchange raised $30.9 billion in 2011, earning the top spot for the third year in a row, while New York raised $30.7 billion. Is it a coincidence that China's exchanges experienced a tremendous rally right up until mid-2015, when, in hindsight, it now seems evident that the bubble burst?

Fast forward to 2014. The United States was once again in the top spot. According to Pricewaterhouse Coopers, IPOs raised $84 billion, the most money generated since 2000. In 2014, Alibaba raised the most money ever in an IPO, at $25 billion. In comparison, in 2012 Facebook raised $16 billion.

Despite the rise in the value of IPOs issued recently, the number of IPOs released of late does not seem to signal alarm that we are close to a top relative to previous market cycles. For example, in the late nineties there were approximately 160 technology IPOs per year; today there are only fifty or so. However, there is a possible answer to this paradox.

Private equity has been responsible for funding many new start-ups today. Cheap money has made it possible for private equity to snap up seemingly attractive deals before they go the usual public route. The real attractiveness of many of these deals has been only temporary, though, considering many of the companies that have gone public recently have dropped below their IPO price. Such declines have not, of course, supported the windfall profits private equity firms had hoped for. Further, 80 percent of new IPOs today have no earnings. The last time we experienced a similar market with 80 percent of IPOs having no earnings was in — you guessed it — 2000.

While researching the number of IPOs being issued on the TSX over the last few years, I uncovered something unexpected. In 2013, the TSX listed 266 IPOs, of which 22 percent were investment products. In 2014, of the 243 listed IPOs, 33 percent were investment products. As of October 2015, conservatively 50 percent of the IPOs were investment products.

What does this suggest? Perhaps the financial industry is more interested in launching new fee-generating assets that attract investment dollars and have no economic value than lending capital to growing businesses that create economic growth and jobs. I have two thoughts on the subject. First, there are fewer businesses seeking capital that qualify as investment worthy, and second, the new investment products being launched have characteristics strikingly similar to prior market tops.

As capital market cycles mature in age, asset managers have an increasingly hard time producing returns that retain and attract the assets of investors who are chasing those same returns. As a result, this forces asset management companies to launch new products that stretch for returns. Many of these also contain greater inherent risks. In particular, I am referring to equity investment products that incorporate equity options. In the bull market of the late 1990s, as asset management companies discovered that returns could be enhanced by selling options, many launched products that included the strategy. This in turn attracted investors who were unprepared when the market abruptly turned. Today I have noticed a similar trend happening. An increasing number of new products being launched have option-selling strategies embedded in their structure. Of course, this is a direct result of our low-interest-rate environment. Such products are focused toward income-seeking investors, but I've seen this behaviour before. *Caveat emptor.*

One final note on IPOs: In Canada, the recent IPO listing of Hydro One common shares appears to be in high demand by institutions and individual investors alike. Typically governments have had poor timing when selling prized assets, but this seems to be an exception. Whether the deal will be successful in the long run is still way too tough for anyone to call. The purpose of the sale was to reduce the debt load the Ontario government accumulated over the past several years. Reducing debt in the short term will lower Ontario's interest payments and put the province in a better fiscal position. We'll see over the coming months if the new Liberal majority will practise restraint or spend like past Liberal governments.

MERGER MANIA

Merger and acquisition (M&A) activity has been clustered in waves. Usually these waves occur in periods of dramatic change, such as deregulation and technological advancement. Transactions usually take place using stock, debt, or both, and, as a result, M&A activity tends to occur when stock valuations are high and access to credit markets is favourable. These factors historically represent the later stage of a bull market.

During the period of 1981 to 1989, a wave of mergers occurred as a result of falling interest rates and easy access to the high-yield debt market pioneered by Michael Milken. The leveraged buyout was a new scheme, allowing small companies to become behemoths overnight by purchasing much larger companies and breaking them up.

This was also the time when corporate raiders identified targets for hostile takeovers. Caught up in the greed and money involved, a number of insiders resorted to nefarious means to identify the next likely takeover candidate in order to profit. Many of the larger insider trading scandals involved a corporate raider named Ivan Boesky.

The period of 1992 to 2001 was fuelled by technological advancement and the internet. The strong bull market leading up to 2000 created many companies with high market valuations. Their high value made it easy for them to use equity to purchase other companies. This period was driven by the need of companies to sustain their growth rates at any cost. Notable events included the meteoric rise and fall of Enron and MCI WorldCom. Hundreds of internet companies with little or no true business models failed and vanished along with their investors' money.

Beginning in 2003, transaction volumes surpassed the heights reached during the internet bubble to all-time highs. The catalyst for the increase in M&A activity can be attributed to globalization and the desire for multinationals to compete worldwide. From 2005 to 2007, financial engineering took a new course and created debt instruments known as CDOs (credit default obligations), which the entire globe participated in. These debt instruments were created by the securitization of mortgages that were packaged and sold as investable debt instruments. Unfortunately, real estate prices didn't go up forever, and the U.S. financial sector caused a global recession that we still haven't fully recovered from today.

Companies have two choices: they can grow by making investments internally — a process known as organic growth — or they can make these investments externally by acquisition. Mergers and acquisitions are motivated by a company's need to stay competitive, create synergies, reach economies of scale, increase market share, tap undeveloped markets, or lower costs of labour. However, the desire to diversify has led some companies to lose sight of their competitive strengths and to expand into businesses where they lack expertise — a trend that is better known as "diworseification."

The real reason executives are motivated to engage in mergers is to maximize the size of the company, rather than create shareholder value. This is not surprising, considering compensation is highly correlated with a company's size. Hubris may also play a part and may stem from assumptions that premium valuations are correct and that executives are somehow smarter than others. The main reason mergers are so easy to initiate at market tops is because these transactions are usually bankrolled by the exchange of the acquiring company's overvalued shares as payment.

The total value of announced takeovers in 2015 passed $4.6 trillion, breaking the record set in 2007. Pfizer's $160 billion purchase of Allergan, struck down by U.S. regulators due to a tax-inversion crackdown, was one of the biggest attempted M&As. Other mega-deals include

Dow Chemical's $130 billion merger with DuPont; Dell's $67 billion deal with storage maker EMC, the biggest tech industry takeover to date; and AnheuserBuschInBev's $110 billion acquisition of SABMiller. All these deals have created chatter that the end of the cycle is near.

Canadian companies have also been involved in their share of deals. CP Rail has attempted to wed twice, first with Norfolk Southern and then with CSX, only to be left standing at the altar due to regulator disapproval. Shaw offered $1.6 billion for Wind Mobile, only to be gobbled up itself for $2.65 billion by Corus Entertainment. Bell's recent bid of $3.9 billion for Manitoba Telecom is just the latest example of what seems like an increasing rush to merge while money is cheap and the markets remain receptive.

As already mentioned, Valeant Pharmaceuticals relied heavily on the junk bond market to fund its business. The company's primary strategy was to make debt-funded acquisitions of other pharmaceutical companies and then jack up prices on acquired products. Valeant's ability to hike prices allowed it to pay expensive multiples for companies and take on excessive debt to pay for them. It seems, however, that some U.S. politicians have a problem with companies taking advantage of sick patients who need the drugs. Outlawing the price increases would result in lower revenue for Valeant and the potential inability to fund its massive debt load. Valeant's troubles were exposed by Citron Research, a short seller who publicly questioned Valeant's revenue recognition and accounting treatment, which has pressured the company's shares and bond prices to distressed levels.

High-yield bond investors should take notice in this low-rate environment — the desperation for yield has created so much demand that not all high-yield bond issues have been created equally. The increased leverage some companies are now carrying could become a problem in the next slowdown. One has to look no further than the energy sector. Since the drop in oil prices that started in mid-2014, defaults among leveraged oil producers are on the rise. Similarly, the emerging markets have been heavy issuers in U.S. dollar–denominated bonds. As the Fed starts to raise rates, further strengthening the U.S. dollar, foreign companies' weakening currencies will boost the burden of funding those U.S. dollar–denominated bonds.

BOND YIELD CURVE

The bond yield curve and what it conveys about the condition of the economy is something to pay close attention to. First, let's determine what a bond yield curve is. By plotting on a graph the one-month, three-month, six-month, one-year, five-year, ten-year, and thirty-year interest rates, we can represent visually the rate of change in yield between the nearest and farthest maturities. Where the yield plot lies (y axis) on the maturity date (x axis) will determine the slope of the curve. A slope can be positive, sloping from bottom left rising to the upper right, or negative, sloping from bottom left to upper right. The slope can also be flat or negative. A negative slope starts at the upper left and falls to the bottom right, either positively or negatively. Refer to Figures 8.3 to 8.9.

An upward-sloping yield curve is usually indicative of a normal economic environment, where short-term rates are lower than long-term rates. A flat or inverted yield curve is usually a cause for concern. A flat or negative yield curve indicates that short-term rates are either equal to or higher than long-term rates. If you think about this for a moment, you soon begin to understand the problem with this scenario. As a fixed-income investor, given the choice of earning the same return, would you rather have your money mature sooner or later? If you're not sure of the answer, refer back to the Power of Compounding in Chapter 3. We expect longer-term maturities to have correspondingly higher yields because investors must bear more risk (inflation, interest rate, opportunity cost). As a financial institution, would you lend money for the same rate you're paying to depositors? Besides fees, this is how banks make most of their profits, commonly known as net interest income. As a business, how are you going to obtain financing or re-finance maturing debt? Banks would only consider making loans to companies with the highest credit quality. One can easily understand how this would slow any economic growth quickly.

How do inverted yield curves materialize in the first place? In the normal course of an economic cycle, as GDP increases, so does the price of goods and services (inflation). As a result, short-term interest rates are increased to slow down economic growth. At this point, one of three outcomes takes place: a desired slowing economy, inflation increasing faster than interest rates, or interest rates rising too quickly. In both of the latter two scenarios, a flat or an inverted yield curve results. In many cases when this occurs, a recession is likely to follow.

In 1990, 1998, and 2007, interest rates were moved higher by the U.S. Federal Reserve to slow the expanding economy. In these particular instances, a recession occurred within the next twelve to eighteen months, preceded by a flat yield curve. The yield curves moved back to being positively sloped when rates were lowered in an attempt to stimulate the economy once again in 1992, 2002, and 2009.

Currently the yield curve is positively sloped, but the question is, when are central banks going to begin to raise rates again?

FIGURE **8.3**
Treasury Yield Curve, January 1990

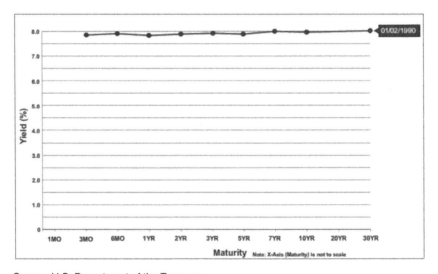

Source: U.S. Department of the Treasury

FIGURE 8.4

Treasury Yield Curve, January 1992

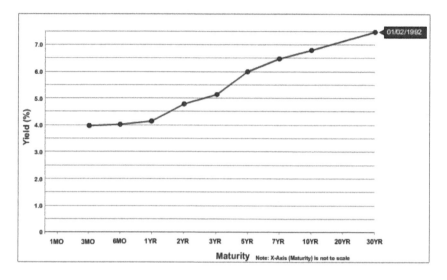

Source: U.S. Department of the Treasury

FIGURE 8.5

Treasury Yield Curve, January 1998

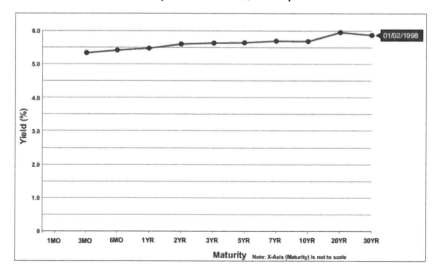

Source: U.S. Department of the Treasury

FIGURE 8.6
Treasury Yield Curve, January 2002

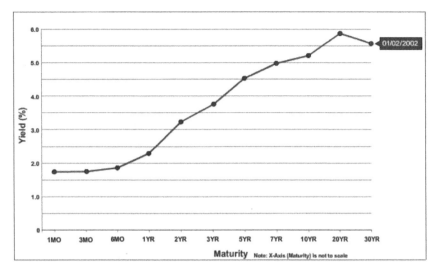

Source: U.S. Department of the Treasury

FIGURE 8.7
Treasury Yield Curve, January 2007

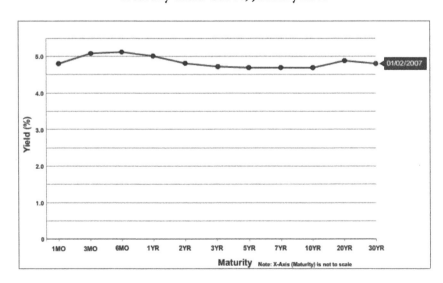

Source: U.S. Department of the Treasury

FIGURE 8.8
Treasury Yield Curve, January 2009

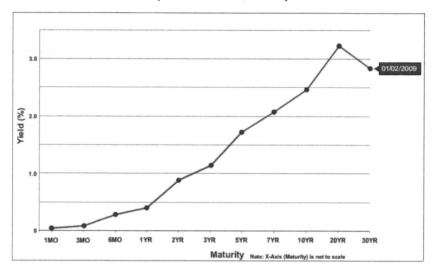

Source: U.S. Department of the Treasury

FIGURE 8.9
Treasury Yield Curve, January 2015

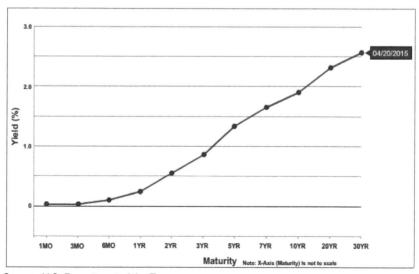

Source: U.S. Department of the Treasury

I should point out that a flat or inverted yield curve does not predict a recession each and every time. In the United States, the yield curve flattened for a short period of time in late 1995 and inverted again in late 2006, both of which were false signals. However, the yield curve can be viewed as a piece of the puzzle that forms the larger picture when used in conjunction with other indicators.

A closer look at the past forty years indicates downturns usually come when the spread between the two- and ten-year treasury yields is zero. Something very different happens when the spread is narrowing but still above zero, as it is now.

After January 1995, the spread had plunged to 85 basis points (100 basis points equals 1 percent), even narrower than it is today. Over the next fifteen months, the S&P 500 jumped more than 10 percent. By November 1998, the spread had collapsed to 39 basis points, less than half what it is now. Over the next two and a half years, the S&P 500 more than doubled.

The take-away: The difference between the two- and ten-year treasuries can be a very useful indicator. But it only becomes useful — signalling severe caution — when it hits zero or when short-term rates rise above long-term rates. Right now investors should look elsewhere for guidance on the outlook.

PRICE-TO-EARNINGS RATIO

The price-to-earnings ratio, or P/E ratio, is an equity valuation multiple. It is defined as market price per share divided by annual earnings per share.

$$P/E = \frac{Price}{Earnings}$$

There are multiple versions of the P/E ratio, but the most popular are the trailing, median, and forward. The trailing P/E uses the most recent twelve-month period of earnings and is the most common meaning of P/E. The median P/E is the statistical mid-point of a series of earning periods that is used to "smooth" out a company's fluctuating earnings due to irregularities such as extraordinary items or seasonality. The forward P/E uses estimated net earnings over the next twelve months. Estimates are typically derived from the average earnings per share published by a group of analysts and can be quite subjective.

Here's an example: If stock A is trading at $50 and the earnings per share for the most recent twelve-month period is $5, then stock A has a P/E ratio of 10 (50 ÷ 5). Put another way, the purchaser of the stock is paying $10 for every dollar of earnings. The ratio demonstrates how many years it takes to cover the price provided earnings remain the same. Companies with losses (negative earnings) or no profit have an undefined P/E ratio, usually designated as N/A or "not applicable."

An investor can tell, from the historical range of high and low P/E ratios, whether a current P/E ratio is a reasonable price to pay for a dollar's worth of earnings. This is not the only indicator an investor should rely on to make an investment decision, but it can be a useful tool along with other metrics to reduce investment blunders. A company's P/E can also be compared to the industry the company is in, the sector the company is in, and the overall market to further determine whether a P/E ratio is high or low.

P/E ratios are highly dependent on the capital structure of a company, meaning how much equity and debt (leverage) a company has. When comparing two companies with identical operations, the company with a moderate amount of debt commonly has a lower P/E than a company with no debt, despite having a slightly higher risk profile, more volatile earnings, and a higher earnings growth rate (if earnings are increasing). Assuming that a company can earn a higher return on the funds borrowed than on the interest expense, the E in the P/E multiple is magnified, lowering the multiple. If the firm has higher levels of debt (leverage) or if profits are declining, it will have a higher P/E ratio than an unleveraged firm.

The P/E ratio of a company is a major focus for many management teams. Since management are usually compensated in company stock or stock options, this form of payment aligns the interests of management with the interests of shareholders. At least this is the belief.

A stock price can increase in one of two ways: through improved earnings, or through an improved multiple the market assigns to those earnings. In turn, the primary driver for multiples, such as the P/E ratio, is higher and more sustained earnings growth.

One activity management can engage in to boost earnings per share is acquiring companies with higher growth prospects, paying for them with cash, debt, or their own stock. Companies with low P/E ratios are usually more open to leveraging their balance sheet for two reasons: it lowers the

P/E ratio further, which means the company looks cheaper than it did before leveraging, and it also improves earnings growth. Both of these factors may drive up the share price.

Since 1900, the average P/E ratio for the S&P 500 index has ranged from 5.72 in January 1918 to 32.92 in January 1999. However, except for some brief periods, from 1920 to 1997 the market P/E ratio was mostly between 10 and 20. The average U.S. equity P/E ratio from 1900 to 2008 was 15. We can deduce from these findings that when the market P/E ratio is close to 10, stocks are considered cheap and should be bought, and when close to 20, are expensive and should be sold. The trailing S&P 500 P/E ratio is currently at 20.

Most U.S. stocks are much more expensive than suggested by the S&P 500 index. The median New York Stock Exchange–listed equity is currently at a post-war record high P/E multiple. In the late 1990s, surging technology stock prices caused the overall S&P 500 to reach record highs even though the median stock's P/E multiple never became excessive. Conversely, today, although the S&P 500 P/E multiple remains far below record highs, median valuations are at a peak. The median U.S. stock began this bull market below twelve times earnings in 2009. In the last five years, however, the median P/E multiple has risen by about two-thirds to slightly more than twenty times earnings. It is important for investors to fully appreciate just how much this bull market has already elevated the valuation landscape.

Record low interest rates throughout this recovery have been producing inflated asset prices. This is true for almost all asset classes, including real estate, fine art, vintage wine, and equities. In order to demonstrate how low interest rates inflate asset prices, consider this real estate example.

In 2007, an income property in my neighbourhood could be purchased for $400,000 and would produce $24,000 of rental income annually. The capitalization rate, often called the cap rate, is the ratio of net operating income to property asset value. In this example the cap rate, or return on investment, was 6 percent (24,000 ÷ 400,000). Another way to think about the cap rate is that it's just the inverse of the price/earnings multiple. Therefore, the P/E would be equal to 16.7, calculated by dividing 400,000 by 24,000. In other words, as the cap rate (return on investment) goes down, the valuation multiple goes up, and vice versa.

Today, the same income property is valued at $875,000. The cap rate or return on investment is 2.7 percent (24,000 ÷ 875,000) and the P/E is 36. Therefore, relative to equities, real estate is extremely overvalued. How will highly inflated asset prices react when interest rates finally start to rise? Many believe that, since interest rates are so low today, they could rise for some time before negatively affecting asset prices. However, if today's widespread extraordinary valuations actually make those assets much more sensitive to interest rates, a real estate correction is certainly conceivable. In any case, investors should proceed with caution.

INSIDER TRANSACTIONS

The most knowledgeable individuals regarding the financial state of a publicly traded company are without a doubt the executive management team and board members. Therefore, it seems appropriate that the buying and selling activity of those individuals would be an indication of their belief in the future of that company. However, more investigation is required in order to determine if this is conclusive. To start, we know that, for a large number of corporate executives, a significant portion of their net worth is in the form of a company's shares. So it seems logical that executives would be net sellers of their company's shares, in order to divest their concentrated wealth as any normal investor would diversify their own portfolio. As a consequence, an insider selling shares does not necessarily indicate negative sentiment. What could indicate a potential issue would be if many insiders were selling large blocks of shares all at the same time. However, even this, taken alone, is not sufficient to determine a potential problem.

An indicator that may provide better proof of the positive outlook of a company's future is insider buying. Once again, the number of insiders buying can also be a representation of the sentiment. One or two would not be significant. Eight or more could be. Also, the manner in which an insider is buying is very important. For example, executive share compensation is granted in the form of options at strike prices, which may be lower than the shares' current market price and, depending on share performance, sometimes much lower. If an executive is exercising options to buy shares at lower than the current market prices and immediately selling, this would not be bullish. If many members of the management team were buying shares in the open market at current market prices, this would be a clearer indication of bullish behaviour. Former Fidelity Investments portfolio manager Peter Lynch, author of *One Up on Wall Street*, said, "There are many reasons for insiders to sell stock, but just one reason to buy: they think the price will rise." Further, he added that insider buying is just one checkmark on an investor's list of buying criteria.

There are a number of sources for researching insider transactions in public companies. In Canada, the TMX group provides insider trade summaries, but only for the most recent trading day. There is likely a subscription-based service with a more robust offering, but I'm only concentrating on the free services. Sedar.com is the Canadian aggregator of public company reporting, but I find it difficult to navigate. Perhaps a subscription does allow for more descriptive searches. In the United States, insidertrading.org is the source for insider information if you know specifically what you are searching for. Edgar is the Sedar equivalent in the United States, and you can find it at www.sec.gov. Yahoo Finance also does a good job of providing the last six months of insider transactions in the left column under the "ownership" heading.

Finally, *Barron's* in the United States offers a proprietary "Insider Transactions Ratio" in its Research Reports section that indicates a bearish or bullish signal depending on the ratio of insider sales to buys. A reading under 12:1 is bullish and one over 20:1 is bearish. Unfortunately, the indicator triggers a confirmation more frequently than corresponding markets move higher or lower.

U.S. PRESIDENTIAL CYCLE

A theory developed by Yale Hirsch states that the U.S. stock markets are weakest in the year following the election of a new U.S. president. According to this theory, after the first year the market improves until the cycle begins again with the next presidential election. As with any market indicator, the theory has not predicted market cycles perfectly, but it does exhibit enough significance that it should not be discounted either. The following is a brief commentary on what market performance occurred surrounding the electoral debut of each U.S. president since the late 1970s.

BARACK OBAMA, 2009–2016

Obama became president in 2009 as the U.S. markets experienced the worst decline since the Great Depression. The cause of the financial crisis was a runaway housing market and the misdeeds of Wall Street firms attempting to capitalize on the frenzy. Many large U.S. financial companies, including Lehman Brothers, Bear Sterns, and Merrill Lynch, either went bankrupt or were taken over. The implications of these events are still felt today, especially in the attempts of central banks around the world to stimulate growth through quantitative easing and prolonged, artificially low interest rate policies.

GEORGE W. BUSH, 2001–2009

Bush took over the presidency as the tech bubble was nearing deflation. The years leading up to Y2K and the spectacular growth of the internet took stock market valuations to extreme levels never seen before. Anyone with an internet idea made a fortune, and most just as quickly gave it back. So, too, did investors who didn't sell.

Just as an economic turnaround was taking hold, the World Trade Center was attacked, and that caused the markets to decline for a second retracement into 2002. The war effort stimulated the U.S. economy and growth once again resumed.

BILL CLINTON, 1993–2001

Bill Clinton benefited from the beginning of an incredible stock market run, which lasted through the 1990s, except for a couple of hiccups between 1994 and 1995 and once again in 1997. In Canada, the banks attempted to merge in the euphoria of the mid-1990s, but they were stopped because of anti-competition concerns.

The market flatlined in 1994–1995 and then resumed its ascent until the fall of 1997, when Long-Term Capital Management (LTCM) had to be bailed out by the U.S. government and emerging markets struggled with currency issues. Two of the three founders of LTCM were Robert Merton and Myron Scholes, who received the Nobel Prize for their work on derivatives pricing. They believed their black box investment model was infallible and that above-average returns were possible indefinitely.

They were proven wrong when Russia decided to default on its debt. They were also highly leveraged to the tune of 30 to 1.

Another notable event was the rise and fall of the Canadian company Nortel. Leading into the year 2000, the markets climbed higher once more, thanks to the tech bubble, until the looming crash a few months later.

GEORGE BUSH SR., 1989–1993

Bush Senior was elected as the markets were topping in the late 1980s. The markets had advanced for eight years straight and were overdue for a correction. In 1990–1991, the United States and Canada experienced a more typical recession, consisting of slowing economic growth and rising unemployment. In particular, real estate prices plunged, as a lot of investors who were speculating in real estate got caught. As Desert Storm was launched, the economy was once again stimulated and the next market cycle began. Was this the beginning of a theme?

RONALD REAGAN, 1981–1989

Reagan began his term when interest rates were reaching their peak of 20 percent. Paul Volcker, head of the Federal Reserve, was instrumental in taming inflation, implementing an extremely aggressive interest rate policy. "Reaganonmics" was the moniker given to the economic policies implemented to lower interest rates after inflation was finally contained. The key drivers were tax cuts, decreased social spending, increased military spending, and deregulation. This period was also the turning point of the secular bond bull market, which has lasted until present day. After the recession ended in 1982, the markets had an impressive rally, until October 19, 1987, otherwise known as Black Monday. Eventually investors, spooked by the one-day drop of 20 percent, saw the opportunity to buy and re-entered the market en masse, helping to grow it until the next recession, which effectively started in 1990.

JIMMY CARTER, 1977–1981

Carter became president in a period confronted with persistent stagflation, a combination of high inflation, high unemployment, and slow growth. Despite the economic uncertainty in the United States, the stock market climbed, since material- and commodity-based companies did well in the inflationary environment. Interest rates ratcheted to a point of choking off the economy in 1980–1981. At their peak, interest rates in Canada were at 21 percent. Gold bullion rallied to $800 per ounce, and it took almost thirty years to reach those levels again, as recently as 2008.

After closer observation, you may notice that the dates of presidential leadership changes coincide with inflection points in market cycles. There were recessions in 1981–1982, 1990–1991, 2001–2002, and 2008–2009. If history holds true, the end of Obama's term makes this an extremely dangerous period for the markets. It is not important whether you believe this theory to be true or not. What is important is that you ignore it at your own peril.

* * *

Studying market cycles for more than thirty-five years has aided me in identifying the repeated behaviours of market peaks and troughs. Understanding investor psychology has helped me recognize the euphoria witnessed just before a market peak and utter emotional exhaustion observed right at the bottom of a market correction. This behaviour is all highly correlated with IPOs, flattening yield curves, equity overvaluation, the behaviour of market participants driving M&A activity, and the inappropriate use of leverage by both individuals and corporations.

Additionally, indications of market inflection points may be linked with cycles such as the U.S. presidential election cycle or Martin Armstrong's pi cycle. What I have attempted to do is provide you with as much evidence as possible. The purpose is to educate you, empower you, and give you tools for profiting from the next bull market.

Most of my discussions up until this point have been theoretical. The next chapter discusses how to put the theory into practice. I start by answering the questions how, what, where, when, and why. Once you know the mechanics of proper execution and timing, the only part remaining is waiting patiently for the opportunity and reaping the rewards.

* * *

There are a number of indicators that signal the top of a bull market. However, they don't always act coincidentally and sometimes may fail to signal a warning at all, while others flash danger. This is what makes the top of a market so hard to determine and explains why so many investors can be unaware that danger even exists.

I have given you enough information in this chapter to connect the dots. There is a clear and present danger. Although the bond yield curve has not flattened, the market's price/earnings multiple is in dangerous territory. Further, the IPO market has cooled, yet margin debt has surpassed its 2007 highs by an enormous amount. Markets can remain irrational for extended periods of time, but eventually gravity takes over and the pendulum swings too far the other way, allowing savvy investors to profit handsomely.

9

THE PLAN

My entire career has been committed to observing, studying, and practising how to succeed at investing in the stock market. For the last seven years I have worked on formulating a wealth-building strategy, and I wrote *How to Profit from the Next Bull Market* in order to share it with you.

Contrary to popular belief, you do not need a Ph.D. in mathematics in order to be a successful investor. If your goal is to make money, the first step is to have a proven plan. What I have outlined in this chapter is my plan, and you may emulate it, modify it, or use the framework to create your own. As you will observe, stock selection is secondary when buying at deep discounted prices (at the right time). These opportunities have presented themselves in every market cycle, most recently in 2002 and 2009, and will soon be available once again. If my thesis is correct, does it not make sense that when a correction does occur, the stocks that were the best performers after the last correction would also be the most likely to recover quickest after the next? What if the stocks I'm referring to demonstrate those very qualities? What if some are not able to survive the next disaster, but because of the ones that do, it doesn't matter? Buying at the right time is what provides the greatest opportunity for investment success. It is more important than any other investment criterion.

I said the first step is to have a "proven" plan because, although anyone can come up with a plan, testing your strategy in the real world is the only way to know if it works. Of course, there are no guarantees. With all investments a certain degree of risk always exists, and the very best investment strategy will still fail if it is not put into practice and followed religiously by the investor. However, a plan does provide rules. Rules give you step-by-step instructions on how to successfully achieve a defined task. Rules also help to remove emotion from the decision-making process. Three of the most harmful character traits that will negatively affect an investor are greed, fear, and impatience. If we know the rules beforehand, there is no need for our emotions to interfere with our decisions. After all, for almost all investors, money can be a very emotional trigger.

Aside from determining its positive expectancy, the evaluation of an investment strategy performs another very important function: it creates certainty.

* * *

I have to add a disclaimer here: All price targets and index levels are subject to change and should be used only for reference and guideline purposes. It's important to remember that past performance is no guarantee of future returns.

How to Prepare

I continue to hear the same narrative from the so-called experts: "It's not timing the market, it's time *in* the market." Well, maybe you don't have the time. Or maybe you would like to make a lot of money sooner rather than later. My argument is that this industry axiom is self-serving and simply not true. No investor has an infinite amount of time to stay in the market. They have to pay attention to cycles if they want to be able to buy low and sell high and so make money. As a result, the most important principle of investing is to buy and sell at the right time to be "the right time in the market."

Of course, all advisors will acknowledge that the key to making money is buying low and selling high. The trick, of course, is knowing when something is "low" and when it is "high." Unfortunately, the advice that is offered is often based on a bad reading of the market. For example, many analysts will constantly increase their price targets on stock. They do this to make you believe that a stock's price is under-valued. In other words, a lot of people in the investment industry are paid to be bullish. Now, it may be true in some instances that this or that stock is undervalued, and so its value will rise. But stocks do not go up forever! According to research by Bespoke Investment Group, "the [fifty] stocks with the best aggregated analyst ratings have performed the worst year-to-date, as of Feb. 8 [2016] [they are] down nearly 17 percent." Continuing with its analysis, BIG observed, "Some of the best-performing stocks — meaning [those that were] the least down (at minus 4.5 percent to minus 7 percent) — were in the three groups with the worst analyst ratings."

So analysts are not always right — especially about stocks always ris-ing in value.

How does this relate to the market today? All of the signs point to an imminent market correction of significant scope. Believing that the bull market we are currently enjoying can continue forever is folly. You need to alter your investment strategy. Failure to do so will result in the kind of losses many experienced in the last major market downturns. As the philosopher George Santayana so adroitly stated, "Those who cannot remember the past are condemned to repeat it."

As I advised earlier, now is the time to withdraw from the equities market. Being 100 percent invested in stocks while on the precipice of a market correction is very dangerous. Ask yourself these two questions: If I withdraw, what is the opportunity cost if the bull market continues? If I don't withdraw, what is the risk if the market does experience a meaning-ful correction? Weighing the risk/reward of each scenario should lead to the conclusion that the risk is far greater than the reward at this point in the market cycle. If you withdraw now and you have a plan, when the time is right you will be in a position to be handsomely rewarded.

What to Buy

The Plan is my recommendation of twenty stocks for you to profit from when the next bull market begins. So your next question most likely is, "Why do you believe that these companies in particular have the great-est opportunity for investment success?" My first response is that you need to invest your money in some asset that is trading at a discount in order to profit. Next, I would suggest that the survival rate of these companies is high given past performance in extremely adverse conditions. I will even outline a worst-case scenario, and the results will amaze you. Furthermore, the companies I've chosen are all leaders in their respective sectors, and most have significant barriers to entry to discourage competitive threats. They all operate in businesses that are easy to understand and in normal market conditions produce tremendous profits. Although the leadership in all of these companies is very capable, as management changes are made the businesses are such that they can operate well as long as they are not interfered with. Further, they all provide products or services that we need or use in our everyday lives.

Past performance is no guarantee, but, as you will learn, these companies were able to generate enormous returns from the last bull market that began in March 2009 and, in some instances, many business cycles. If my theory is correct, when the next bull market arrives, your reward will be financial security and a comfortable retirement, the goal of reading this book and putting it into action.

My reasoning for choosing these twenty stocks was based on two things: the fundamental soundness of each business, and my personal experience of owning some of them in client portfolios for more than twenty years. Since these stocks are covered extensively by many firms whose reports are readily available, in the Appendix I have provided a less-common but easy-to-understand SWOT (strengths, weaknesses, opportunities, threats) analysis of each company, as opposed to the typical "number crunch" report. By understanding a company's business this way, you can more easily assess its merits and its ability to overcome adversity. As you will observe, even the best companies need to constantly be aware of who is a potential threat in this disruptive age of ever-changing technology and social media.

Most importantly, I have established price targets that represent fabulous entry points and are low enough to provide incredible profits if purchased close to those levels. How did I arrive at these price targets? They are the prices that the stocks were trading at in the spring of 2009. History has a way of repeating itself, stocks tend to gravitate to where they have been in the past, and this is true for both the lows and the highs.

TABLE 9.1
The Plan All-Star Team

Stock	Symbol	Exchange	Price Target
Alimentation Couche-Tarde Inc.	ATD.B	TSX	$4.05
Brookfield Asset Management Inc.	BAM.A	TSX	$10.28
Canadian Pacific Railway	CP	TSX	$36.90
Canadian Tire Corporation	CTC.A	TSX	$42.80
Enbridge Inc.	ENB	TSX	$19.06
Magna International Inc.	MG	TSX	$7.80
National Bank	NA	TSX	$20.50
Royal Bank	RY	TSX	$35.25
Telus Corporation	T	TSX	$16.67
Toronto Dominion Bank	TD	TSX	$20.63
Apple Inc.	AAPL	NASDAQ	$14.50
Boeing Co.	BA	NYSE	$32.55
Capital One Financial Corp.	COF	NYSE	$11.34
Costco Wholesale Corp.	COST	NASDAQ	$44.83
The Home Depot Inc.	HD	NYSE	$22.16
MasterCard Inc.	MA	NYSE	$15.55
Nike Inc.	NKE	NYSE	$11.26
Novo Nordisk	NVO	NYSE	$9.06
Starbucks Corporation	SBUX	NASDAQ	$5.58
Walt Disney Co.	DIS	NYSE	$17.45

Table 9.2 lists the percentage sector weightings represented in The Plan. Upon further observation, it seems consistent with prior market rebounds that the chosen equities are ideally allocated for a strong market recovery and provide full diversification.

TABLE 9.2

Percentage Sector Weighting of Plan Stocks

Sector	%
Consumer Discretionary	30
Financials	25
Consumer Staples	10
Industrial	10
Technology	10
Energy	5
Health Care	5
Telecommunication	5
	100

As Table 9.3 shows, $1 million invested in these companies in the spring of 2009 would have appreciated to $5.45 million by the summer of 2015. This equates to a return of over 445 percent, or 27 percent compounded annually.

TABLE 9.3

The Plan Appreciation, 2009–2015

	Low	High	Return	Amount	Profit/Loss
ATD.B	4.05	53.52	1,221.5%	50,000	610,740.74
BAM.A	10.28	43.13	319.6%	50,000	159,776.26
CP	36.9	205.8	457.7%	50,000	228,861.79
CTC.A	42.8	132.3	209.1%	50,000	104,556.07
ENB	19.06	55.81	192.8%	50,000	96,406.09
MG	7.8	71.22	813.1%	50,000	406,538.46

	Low	High	Return	Amount	Profit/Loss
NA	20.5	48.6	137.1%	50,000	68,536.59
RY	35.25	78.24	122.0%	50,000	60,978.72
T	16.67	41.08	146.4%	50,000	73,215.36
TD	20.63	54.22	162.8%	50,000	81,410.57
AAPL	14.5	126.92	775.3%	50,000	387,655.17
BA	32.55	142.29	337.1%	50,000	168,571.43
COF	11.34	87.49	671.5%	50,000	335,758.38
COST	44.83	137.23	206.1%	50,000	103,055.99
HD	22.16	110.01	396.4%	50,000	198,217.51
MA	15.55	93.3	500.0%	50,000	250,000.00
NKE	11.26	51.67	358.9%	50,000	179,440.50
NVO	9.06	56.23	520.6%	50,000	260,320.09
SBUX	5.58	52.27	836.7%	50,000	418,369.18
DIS	17.45	110.18	531.4%	50,000	265,702.01
				1,000,000	4,458,110.89

I know what you're thinking. You're skeptical — this is absurd because it's history, and past performance is no guarantee of future returns. You are absolutely correct, but I left out one important argument that is instrumental in reinforcing my thesis of buying stocks at the right time. Hypothetically speaking, what if I told you that, even if the five best-performing stocks of the twenty had gone bankrupt because of poor stock selection, the remaining fifteen would still have managed to earn over 12 percent compounded annually? Would that make you reconsider?

TABLE 9.4
The Plan All-Star Team with Five Top Performers Removed

	Low	High	Return	Amount	Profit/Loss
ATD.B	4.05	0	−100.0%	50,000	−50,000.00
BAM.A	10.28	43.13	319.6%	50,000	159,776.26
CP	36.9	205.8	457.7%	50,000	228,861.79
CTC.A	42.8	132.3	209.1%	50,000	104,556.07
ENB	19.06	55.81	192.8%	50,000	96,406.09
MG	7.8	0	−100.0%	50,000	−50,000.00
NA	20.5	48.6	137.1%	50,000	68,536.59
RY	35.25	78.24	122.0%	50,000	60,978.72
T	16.67	41.08	146.4%	50,000	73,215.36
TD	20.63	54.22	162.8%	50,000	81,410.57
AAPL	14.5	0	−100.0%	50,000	−50,000.00
BA	32.55	142.29	337.1%	50,000	168,571.43
COF	11.34	0	−100.0%	50,000	−50,000.00
COST	44.83	137.23	206.1%	50,000	103,055.99
HD	22.16	110.01	396.4%	50,000	198,217.51
MA	15.55	93.3	500.0%	50,000	250,000.00
NKE	11.26	51.67	358.9%	50,000	179,440.50
NVO	9.06	56.23	520.6%	50,000	260,320.09
SBUX	5.58	0	−100.0%	50,000	−50,000.00
DIS	17.45	110.18	531.4%	50,000	265,702.01
				1,000,000	2,049,048.97

Many of the stocks selected in The Plan have endured prior market corrections and thrived. As a result, even if a few don't survive the next correction, your portfolio will still perform extremely well.

This illustration is proof that The Plan is capable of producing astonishing investment returns. While investing in these stocks between 2009 and 2015 would have delivered great results for you, it's important to keep in mind that these are not the only stocks capable of delivering great returns. Buying at the right time is even more important than individual stock selection.

Listed in Table 9.5 are the actual individual returns of The Plan stock portfolio from January 4, 2007, to March 9, 2009. Some explanation is required in order to interpret what may appear to be major discrepancies. At first glance, it may look like Apple, Novo Nordisk, and MasterCard did not experience a loss in value during this period. That would not be entirely correct. In fact, they did drop considerably from their highs, highs that were reached a lot further into the market correction in 2008.

TABLE 9.5
The Plan's Individual Performance in the Last Correction in 2007–2009

	Return
COF	−88.7%
SBUX	−76.5%
MG	−72.5%
BA	−66.4%
BAM.A	−60.4%
HD	−55.1%
DIS	−54.1%
TD	−50.2%
RY	−48.2%
ATD.B	−47.4%
CP	−46.2%
NA	−45.7%
CTC.A	−43.1%
T	−40.2%
COST	−28.9%
NKE	−21.8%
ENB	−19.1%
AAPL	−0.4%
NVO	4.9%
MA	40.9%

Referring back to The Plan's individual largest price decliners in the last market correction — Capital One, Starbucks, and Magna — we find that even though they were the worst decliners, they were also the best performers in the recovery. If you held these stocks from peak to trough in the last cycle, what return would have been required in order to get back to break-even?

TABLE 9.6

Rate of Return Required to Break-Even

	Loss	Break-Even
COF	−88.7%	733%
SBUX	−76.5%	316%
MG	−72.5%	257%

Now for the obvious question: Why would you want to experience that emotional roller coaster when you could simply wait, buy at the bottom, and capture those enormous returns without the initial loss? Cognitive dissonance may be one answer. This is where our attitude and behaviour are in conflict with one another. As investors, our thought is that we don't want to miss the next big market gain. Yet we don't want to feel the emotional stress of losing a lot of money. We remember what 2008–2009 felt like and don't want to experience that again. So we don't do anything, and we remain invested. This conflict is what causes the dissonance: we don't want to lose money, but we remain invested, like a smoker who knows smoking causes cancer yet continues to do it.

Another possible explanation is the endowment effect. Humans are supposed to be rational, but experiments have proven that we value things more highly when we already have them in our possession. An even more obvious explanation is "FOMO" — fear of missing out. Don't be fooled; the probability of a major correction grows larger each day. Here is the bottom line: if you don't want to feel emotional despondence from the loss in value of your investments, you need to take appropriate action now.

TRADING TECHNIQUES TO USE

A number of techniques are used by professional investors for trade execution, but these techniques also play an important role in their overall strategies by assisting with the mechanics of investing. I will explore a few of the more common ones: scaling, trailing stops, and profit targets. The Plan employs these techniques.

Scaling, otherwise known as dollar-cost averaging, is the term used to describe the accumulation or reduction in the quantity of an underlying asset. It is used as a systematic approach to averaging into a buy price or out of a sell price. When scaling into a position, a buyer adds incrementally to an existing position as the market price moves in the profitable direction of the trade. A buyer who is scaling out of a position incrementally decreases an existing position once a sell target price has been reached.

A trailing stop is a dynamic order that moves with the market, going up with new highs (longs) or down with new lows (shorts) in order to preserve some predetermined proportion of the open trade profit (for example, at a set percentage below the market for a long position or above the market for a short position). The trailing stop is placed in a manner in which it advances in the direction of a profitable market move during the life of the trade. That is, a trailing stop to protect a long position will move up as the market advances and down to protect a short as the market declines. The ideal trailing stop preserves as much open trading profit as possible while at the same time providing enough breathing room to accommodate the price movement that is a part of all trades. The goal of a trailing stop is to exit the trade when the main thrust of the trade is ended.

The other way to protect profits is to "take" profits when a price target has been reached. A profit target is an unconditional exit of a trade with a locked-in profit at some predetermined price. Limit orders are an effective way to establish new positions or exit at an obtained price target. I cannot stress enough the importance of always using limit orders when placing a trade, especially in volatile markets. The purpose is to ensure that you don't pay too much when making a purchase and that you receive a fair price when you're selling.

The most positive aspect of a profit target is that, once the desired profit is realized, it is captured immediately. Therefore, it cannot be lost. The negative aspect occurs when a profit is taken and the market continues to advance beyond the target. The potential gains are lost because the profit target has closed out the position. Which reminds me of the investment proverb: "Bulls make money, bears make money, but pigs get slaughtered." In other words, greed can turn profitable trades into losses faster than your ability to act in a timely manner.

WHEN TO BUY

When the correction starts gaining momentum, the media will be playing into the fears of the public. Emphasis will be placed on the investor's loss of retirement savings, jobs, and financial security. The finger pointing will begin. The blame will be directed toward the central bankers, politicians, and corporate greed. We will likely experience a growing number of public protests and increased social unrest, which will all make front page headlines. The indicators mentioned throughout the book, such as the market indices and the volatility index, will begin to move toward target levels. We should start to see the companies with weaker balance sheets, or the ones exposed to any black swan events, implode. Recall what happened to Bear Sterns, Lehman Brothers, Merrill Lynch, and Wachovia Bank during the financial crisis. Although a bear market usually lasts between twelve and eighteen months, each situation is different and must be assessed in real time. I will be providing regular updates at www.thenextbullmarket.com.

Most market experts will recommend staying invested, while others, more emotionally driven, may suggest selling everything and moving to cash or bonds, which would be the correct action to take, but doing so at that stage in the cycle would be poor timing, since considerable losses would have already been incurred by then. If you have read this book in time and taken the appropriate action, you will have avoided most of this unpleasant experience.

The Plan preparation should begin to take effect. This includes having capital readily available, accounts accessible, stocks chosen, and their respective price targets known. To provide a reference point where we could potentially expect major indices to drop to, I have created a chart of the last two corrections and their respective index levels.

TABLE 9.7
Stock Index Target Levels

		1	2	3	Target Levels	Average
2009	Dow	8,000	7,000	8,000	8,000	9,000
	S&P 500	800	700	800	800	975
	NASDAQ	1,400	1,300	1,400	1,400	1,700
	S&P/TSX	9,000	7,500	9,000	9,000	8,500
2002	Dow	10,000	8,500	10,000	10,000	
	S&P 500	1,150	1,000	1,150	1,150	
	NASDAQ	2,000	1,500	2,000	2,000	
	S&P/TSX	8,000	6,500	8,000	8,000	

Headings 1 to 3 represent the capitulation phase of a market bottom. This period is usually characterized by panic selling and large volumes. A one-day crisis event will typically occur in which huge volumes of shares are traded and the market displays an extremely large trading range, with opening and closing market levels that are close or equal. This entire bottoming process can last anywhere between one and four months, with capitulation being the final event. These are our goal posts!

Due to the speed at which companies are being disrupted today because of technology and other equally powerful forces, when the time does arrive to enact The Plan, do your research and check the current status of the companies in the All-Star Team, and talk to your financial advisor. Or you could contact me, and I'll let you know where the members of the All-Star Team sit at the moment. Alternatively, take a look at my website, www.thenextbullmarket.com.

Our objective is to start scaling into the twenty stocks, with equal percentages allocated to each. The price targets established for the individual equities are the previous lows of 2009. Although these price targets are not written in stone, they provide a good reference point for our approximate target prices. I anticipate that after we buy the first installment, price levels may then dip further. Remember, we are not trying to pick the bottom; we are trying to dollar-cost-average and avoid being influenced by our emotions.

The aim is to be fully invested in either three or four installments. The choice is yours. If choosing three, then each stock purchase weighting should equal 1.67 percent of the total portfolio value. This in turn would equal sixty transactions over three installment periods. If choosing four installments, then each stock purchase weighting should equal 1.25 percent of the total portfolio value. This would equate to eighty transactions over the four installment periods. Anything less would be foolhardy and anything more would be too onerous.

There are a couple of potential "hiccups" that can make executing this strategy somewhat more difficult: the possibility of a bear trap or a double dip. These can occur after an initial thrust off a recessionary market low. Knowing that this may occur may be enough to keep you from making a poor decision. The reason it happens is that there is considerable doubt whether policy makers will make the right choices in order to stabilize and reboot the economy. Don't let these spoilers scare you out of the market. They will usually happen shortly after the first bottom is made and won't last for long, since the smart money will soon start to find its way back into the market. Remember I made a reference earlier to a proven plan? Well, this is it! The proof that the strategy is working is that, if you have executed The Plan properly, the portfolio should be profitable. If not, be patient. You've bought at deeply discounted prices and will be making money shortly.

USING LEVERAGE

If the use of leverage isn't recommended in almost every instance of investing in equities, then the opposite must also be true — there must be a time when it is appropriate. The answer to that is unequivocally yes. That time is exactly the same as when I'm recommending you buy the stocks in The Plan. However, there need to be additional rules put in place to ensure the odds of success are tipped securely in your favour.

If you are an investor who is not averse to using leverage, please take care in applying these principles. Leverage is capable of producing great rewards but equally great heartache. It is a very powerful tool, but the negative effects of unsuccessful uses of leverage can be devastating. It is the number one cause of destruction of an individual investor's portfolio, and as a consequence it has the potential to ruin lives as well. Let me be perfectly clear: the unsuccessful use of leverage can bankrupt you, and in the end you may owe much more than what you lost of your own money. It can cost you your home, break up your marriage, and split your family. Leverage is responsible for destroying many companies and devastating the lives of their employees and those employees' families.

In the mid-nineties, Nick Leeson worked as a futures floor trader in Asia for Barings Bank. When a co-worker got caught in a small trade loss, Nick's attempt to recoup the loss resulted in the bank's eventual collapse. Nick's intentions were good, but the results were devastating. Leverage is a dangerous tool in the wrong hands and when used inappropriately. Unfortunately, that is the case in most instances. Despite the odds, however, investors still risk using leverage in the pursuit of financial independence.

For those who are willing to accept the risks and, even more importantly, have the discipline and secure cash flow to cover the borrowing costs, I will do my best to provide the rules of engagement. Most investors use leverage incorrectly, so let's begin by discussing how this happens. Leverage should *never* be used when

- the stock market is one year or more off the bottom of the last secular bear market;
- you are solicited by your financial advisor (only if the first point is applicable);
- you are unemployed;
- a tax deduction is the motivation;
- a family member tries to persuade you;
- someone tells you how much money they are making;
- the stock market is at or close to all-time highs;
- the stock market has been two years or more without a meaningful correction; or
- *it feels good!*

These rules of leverage use work because they help investors avoid making poor decisions. When investors make emotional decisions, those decisions very seldom work out in the investors' favour. The same lack of success is true for the emotional decisions of financial advisors as well. You may be surprised that financial advisors make emotional decisions. You shouldn't be! Are we not human? We sometimes let our emotions get the best of us.

Unfortunately, such decisions are most often associated with recommendations to use leverage. That being said, in my career I have never met a client who has had a good experience with a prior advisor's leverage recommendation. In hindsight, it has always seemed to come at the worst possible time to be starting a leverage strategy. Why do advisors recommend leverage to their clients when the markets are at or near all-time highs? Because they are acting on their emotions and it feels good, and the clients buy in because they have been making money and they feel good too.

Of course, an advisor's motivation is likely to be self-serving. A client's use of leverage usually results in a larger dollar amount being invested, and that means a bigger commission for the advisor. Just as the CEO of a corporation is motivated by compensation, so too are advisors.

Leverage should only be initiated at the bottom of a bear market inflection point. Much of the subject matter of this book is dedicated to, as closely as possible, identifying that period. If, despite all of the dangers, you are still interested in leveraging, then each position in the portfolio can be increased from 5 percent to 10 percent. I know that it may be possible to obtain greater leverage from the portfolio, but it is best to keep it at 50 percent. This is not as aggressive a policy as is possible, but it will provide a cushion in the event of any adverse market conditions.

Once again, you should scale into the additional positions in six installments. The first two installments should each be at a 1.25 percent weighting and the additional four installments at 0.625 percent. The equity prices can be used as a gauge for when to initiate the additional shares purchases. For example, each time the equity position goes up by 25 to 50 percent, initiate the next installment. This is a blend of both art and science and will depend on each equity's performance. Remember that put writing is an effective strategy for scaling into positions and generating cash flow to help with interest carrying charges (see Advanced Strategies). Again, this is both an art and a science.

So, knowing the potential benefits and risks of using leverage and knowing how to use it to scale into the market, the question becomes when to apply it. As I've said before, you want to buy at the bottom of a bear market. But buying at the bottom of a bear market correction is much harder than doing so at the top of a bull market. It feels horrible! You may be worried about your job. The media is bombarding us with doom and gloom. The world seems to be falling apart. Still, this is your opportunity. If you can keep your emotions out of the decision-making process, the probability of success goes up dramatically. The simple key to making money in the stock market is buying low and selling high. However, this is much harder to do in practice. If it were easy, everyone would make money in the stock market.

Now that we have identified the right time to use leverage — notice I didn't say that we've identified "how to time the market" or "what the right amount of time in the market is" — let's look at the numbers. When borrowing to invest, the break-even point is higher than 0 percent, but not as high as the cost of borrowing, because the interest expense is tax deductible. It's important to remember two of the important benefits of using leverage to invest: the ability to defer and lower taxation of capital gains. As time goes by, the compounding of money reduces the rate of return required to break even.

Table 9.8 is a snapshot of the mechanics of a leverage loan over a one-year period, for illustration. Any return above 4.5 percent would be profitable despite the loan interest rate of 6 percent.

TABLE 9.8
Leverage Break-Even Return Scenario

Loan Amount		$ 10,000
Interest Cost	6.0%	$600
Marginal Tax Rate	40.0%	
Deduction		$240
After-Tax Cost		$360
Investment Return	4.5%	$450
Capital Gains Tax	50.0%	$90
Profit/Loss		—
Rate of Return		0.0%

The most common methods for accessing leverage are through a term loan, a line of credit, or a margin account. Security may be required to qualify for a loan, but this means that the cost to borrow would most likely be lower. For an investment loan, the investment being purchased may sometimes be held as security against the loan. A loan requires payments that blend interest and principal so that, as time passes, the loan is paid off.

The security on a line of credit is usually real estate, and many financial institutions allow for interest-only payments. The interest rate charged on a home equity line of credit is the lowest among borrowing options and also eliminates the risk of a margin call.

A brokerage firm will allow you to borrow money for additional buying power from the margin you have deposited into a margin account. The interest rate on a margin account is usually a bit higher than that on a secured line of credit. As well, if the balance of a margin account drops below a minimum amount, a margin call is made and additional funds are required from the investor to bring the account back into good standing.

How much can you afford to borrow? We can answer this question by reverse engineering the equation. First, determine the size of monthly payment you can comfortably afford. For illustration, let's say $1,000. A term loan should be amortized over five years maximum. Why five years? Because this is the maximum length of time you have to conservatively stay fully invested in a market cycle.

Once you've figured out how much you can afford to pay, the next step is to determine the rate of interest on the loan. It's wisest to be safe and use a best- and worst-case scenario in order to keep the payments within your comfort zone — say, for instance, 5 percent and 8 percent. At a 5 percent interest rate and loan amount of $50,000, the monthly payment is $943.56. At 8 percent, a $50,000 loan payment is $1,013.82, which is over the maximum payment limit. At this point, you may either reduce the loan amount or accept the risk of the additional funding requirement. With a monthly payment of $500, the maximum loan amount would be $25,000. Again working backward, at 5 percent the monthly payment would be $471.78. At 8 percent, the payment would be $506.91, over the $500 payment limit. Again, decide what the best course of action is for your comfort level. Reduce the loan or accept the additional risk.

To determine the loan amount on an interest-only payment, the amount you can obtain increases dramatically — but so does the risk. Remember, the term loan is being paid back over time. With an interest-only loan, the full amount must be paid back at the end. Assuming a $1,000 monthly interest payment, the annual interest expense would be $12,000. Dividing the interest payments of $12,000 by 5 percent, you obtain a principal of $240,000. At a more conservative 8 percent, $12,000 divided by 8 percent is $150,000. With a monthly interest payment of $500, the annual interest expense is $6,000. Divide that number by 5 percent and you obtain a principal of $120,000. At 8 percent, the loan amount is $75,000. Remember, these are merely guidelines, but they should not be taken lightly. Your risk tolerance and ability to carry the loan are your first and only priorities.

THE EDGE

The "edge" is a term used in games of chance to describe the advantage over other competitors or the house. Casinos, for instance, always have the edge. However, the stock market is not a casino, although many like to say it is. That's because they don't know the secret.

Having the edge is not a 100 percent guarantee, but mathematicians know that over time the one who has the edge wins. The edge I've been referring to throughout the book is asymmetrical returns. So what is an asymmetrical return anyway? I'm glad you asked!

To answer the question, I first need to define symmetrical. Symmetrical distributions are said to be balanced — to have symmetry. Also called a normal distribution, its pattern is recognized by its shape: the Gaussian bell curve. Investment risk and return profiles are often plotted in a histogram shaped like a bell curve for analysis of the data. Essentially, what this tells us is that there is an equal chance of either a profit or a loss. Figure 9.1 is an example of a normal distribution bell curve.

FIGURE 9.1
Normal Distribution (Bell) Curve

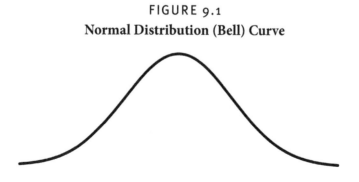

Fortunately for us, market returns do not present the perfect balance of symmetry most academic theories assume in modern financial studies. This is exactly the reason why investors are shocked when they experience larger-than-expected losses and get euphoric after larger-than-usual gains. The net result of symmetry over time is no investment return.

An asymmetric distribution is one that is skewed to the right or the left. The distribution data is placed in a histogram, but instead of a bell-curve shape, with the majority of the data points in the middle of the distribution, the asymmetric distribution has more data on the left, right, or both. The following diagram is an example of an asymmetrical curve skewed to the right.

FIGURE 9.2
Asymmetrical Curve Skewed to the Right

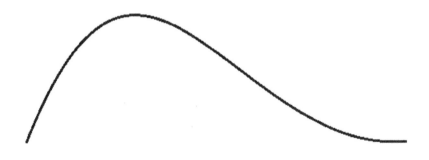

Stock market returns are asymmetric in that they have what are known as "fat tails." As Figure 9.2 demonstrates, the fat tail to the right exhibits a much greater chance of returns than the tail to the left. This is the opportunity we are waiting for. If you were to flip this graph over on the y axis, with the fat tail on the left side, as in Figure 9.3, there would be a greater possibility for returns to the left. This is where I believe we are in the market cycle right now.

FIGURE 9.3
Asymmetrical Curve Skewed to the Left

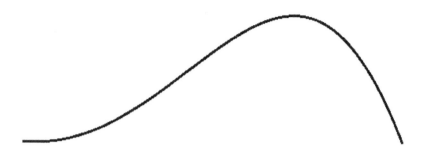

Because asymmetric return distributions develop on both sides, investors are often lured into a false sense of security. The problem is that very large gains often lead investors into complacency and over-optimism right when they need to do the opposite to have any chance of avoiding a devastating loss. Of course, this type of investor usually doesn't believe timing is important, which leads to their full participation in the roller coaster swings that occur across full market cycles of bull and bear markets. If this is you, please do what is necessary to avoid the painful losses that will be experienced when the next correction occurs. It is getting close. If you do, you will be well positioned to participate in The Plan when the asymmetrical distribution curve flips the other way and the market rebounds.

10

MARKET WISDOM

I wrote this book as a blueprint for individuals and families who want to become financially secure. I wanted to share the secret of how to successfully invest in the stock market with a high probability of earning asymmetrical returns. More importantly, I wanted investors to know that you didn't have to "trade" in order to do it. In fact, *How to Profit from the Next Bull Market* is the antithesis of a trading book. If you are correctly applying The Plan I have shared, trading is not only unnecessary, but in fact, engaging in frequent trades may even detract from The Plan's full potential.

Now, I am not suggesting that nothing can be learned from a trader's insights. Quite the contrary — I think there is a great deal to be learned from them. This is why I am including a few of the more famous traders' rules for trading success and avoiding costly mistakes. As you read through them, you will notice that many of them repeat the same lessons. This shows that human beings tend to make the same mistakes, and these are the ones that we should particularly heed. You will also notice that I have placed some rules in italics. These are the rules that I believe are of particular use for investors applying The Plan or that I have already mentioned in this book.

The first set of rules comes from Gerald Loeb. Mr. Loeb was a founding partner of E.F. Hutton & Co., a highly regarded investment firm in New York. Loeb first became known for his book *The Battle for Investment Survival*, which was popular during the Great Depression and is still considered a classic today. The Wall Street Crash of 1929 greatly affected

Loeb's investing style, and in his 1971 book he viewed the market as a battlefield, which offered a contrarian investing viewpoint.

1. The most important single factor in shaping security markets is public psychology.
2. To make money in the stock market you either have to be ahead of the crowd or very sure they are going in the same direction for some time to come.
3. *Accepting losses is the most important single investment device to insure safety of capital.*
4. The difference between the investor who year in and year out procures for himself a final net profit, and the one who usually in the red is not entirely a question of superior selection of stocks or superior timing. Rather, it is also a case of knowing how to capitalize successes and curtail failures.
5. One useful fact to remember is that the most important indications are made in the early stages of a broad market move. Nine times out of ten the leaders of an advance are the stocks that make new highs ahead of the averages.
6. There is a saying, "A picture is worth a thousand words." Using the same idea, you can say that a profit is worth more than endless alibis or explanations … prices and trends are really the best and simplest "indicators" you can find.
7. Profits can be made safely only when the opportunity is available and not just because they happen to be desired or needed.
8. *Willingness and ability to hold funds uninvested while awaiting real opportunities is a key to success in the battle for investment survival.*
9. In addition to many other contributing factors of inflation or deflation, a very great factor is the psychological. The fact that people think prices are going to advance or decline very much contributes to their movement, and the very momentum of the trend itself tends to perpetuate itself.
10. Most people, especially investors, try to get a certain percentage return, and actually secure a minus yield when

properly calculated over the years. Speculators risk less and have a better chance of getting something, in my opinion.

11. I feel all relevant factors, important and otherwise, are registered in the market's behaviour, and, in addition, the action of the market itself can be expected under most circumstances to stimulate buying or selling in a manner consistent enough to allow reasonably accurate forecasting of news in advance of its actual occurrence.

12. *You don't need analysts in a bull market, and you don't want them in a bear market.*

The second set of commandments comes from the fictionalized biography of Jesse Livermore. Written in 1923 by Edwin Lefèvre, *Reminiscences of a Stock Operator* remains the most widely read and highly recommended investment book. It is filled with observational gems about the markets and trading and is a suggested fun read on my recommended reading list.

1. Nothing new ever occurs in the business of speculating or investing in securities and commodities.

2. Money cannot consistently be made trading every day or every week during the year.

3. *Don't trust your own opinion, and back your judgment until the action of the market itself confirms your opinion.*

4. Markets are never wrong — opinions often are.

5. *The real money made in speculating has been in commitments showing in profit right from the start.*

6. *As long as a stock is acting right, and the market is right, do not be in a hurry to take profits.*

7. One should never permit speculative ventures to run into investments.

8. The money lost by speculation alone is small compared with the gigantic sums lost by so-called investors who have let their investments ride.

9. Never buy a stock because it has had a big decline from its previous high.

10. Never sell a stock because it seems high-priced.

11. I become a buyer as soon as a stock makes a new high on its movement after having had a normal reaction.
12. *Never average losses.*
13. *The human side of every person is the greatest enemy of the average investor or speculator.*
14. Wishful thinking must be banished.
15. *Big movements take time to develop.*
16. It is not good to be too curious about all the reasons behind price movements.
17. *It is much easier to watch a few than many.*
18. If you cannot make money out of the leading active issues, you are not going to make money out of the stock market as a whole.
19. The leaders of today may not be the leaders of two years from now.
20. Do not become completely bearish or bullish on the whole market because one stock in some particular group has plainly reversed its course from the general trend.
21. *Few people ever make money on tips. Beware of inside information. If there was easy money lying around, no one would be forcing it into your pocket.*

Bernard Baruch, the third trader on my list, was an American financier, stock investor, philanthropist, statesman, and political consultant. By 1903 Baruch had his own brokerage firm and had gained a reputation as "The Lone Wolf of Wall Street" because of his refusal to join any financial house. By 1910 he had become one of Wall Street's best-known financiers. He amassed a fortune before the age of thirty speculating in the sugar market.

1. Don't speculate unless you can make it a full-time job.
2. *Beware of barbers, beauticians, waiters — of anyone — bringing gifts of "inside" information or "tips."*
3. *Before you buy a security, find out everything you can about the company, its management and competitors, its earnings and possibilities for growth.*

4. *Don't try to buy at the bottom and sell at the top. This can't be done — except by liars.*
5. *Learn how to take your losses quickly and cleanly. Don't expect to be right all the time. If you have made a mistake, cut your losses as quickly as possible.*
6. Don't buy too many different securities. Better have only a few investments that can be watched.
7. Make a periodic reappraisal of all your investments to see whether changing developments have altered their prospects.
8. Study your tax position to know when you can sell to greatest advantage.
9. Always keep a good part of your capital in a cash reserve. Never invest all your funds.
10. Don't try to be a jack of all investments. Stick to the field you know best.

The fourth market trader, P. Arthur Huprich, serves as the chief market technician and portfolio manager at Day Hagan Asset Management in Sarasota, Florida. Mr. Huprich has been an analyst in the financial services industry for nearly thirty years. He has been a frequent guest lecturer at Loyola College of Maryland and Schiller International University – Florida campus, and has provided commentary for news organizations such as *Investor's Business Daily*, *The Technical Analyst*, and the *Washington Post*.

1. Commandment #1: "Thou Shall Not Trade Against the Trend."
2. *Portfolios heavy with under-performing stocks rarely outperform the stock market!*
3. *There is nothing new on Wall Street. There can't be because speculation is as old as the hills. Whatever happens in the stock market today has happened before and will happen again, mostly due to human nature.*
4. Sell when you can, not when you have to.
5. Bulls make money, bears make money, and "pigs" get slaughtered.
6. *We can't control the stock market. The very best we can do is to try to understand what the stock market is trying to tell us.*

7. *Understanding mass psychology is just as important as understanding fundamentals and economics.*

8. *Learn to take losses quickly, don't expect to be right all the time, and learn from your mistakes.*

9. Don't think you can consistently buy at the bottom or sell at the top. This can rarely be consistently done.

10. When trading, remain objective. Don't have a preconceived idea or prejudice. Said another way, "The great names in trading all have the same trait: an ability to shift on a dime when the shifting time comes."

11. Any dead fish can go with the flow. Yet, it takes a strong fish to swim against the flow. In other words, what seems "hard" at the time is usually, over time, right.

12. Even the best looking chart can fall apart for no apparent reason. Thus, never fall in love with a position but instead remain vigilant in managing risk and expectations. Use volume as a confirming guidepost.

13. When trading, if a stock doesn't perform as expected within a short time period, either close it out or tighten your stop-loss point.

14. *As long as a stock is acting right and the market is "in-gear," don't be in a hurry to take a profit on the whole position. Scale out instead.*

15. Never let a profitable trade turn into a loss, and never let an initial trading position turn into a long-term one because it is at a loss.

16. Don't buy a stock simply because it has had a big decline from its high and is now a "better value"; wait for the market to recognize "value" first.

17. *Don't average trading losses, meaning don't put "good" money after "bad." Adding to a losing position will lead to ruin. Ask the Nobel laureates of Long-Term Capital Management.*

18. *Human emotion is a big enemy of the average investor and trader. Be patient and unemotional. There are periods where traders don't need to trade.*

19. Wishful thinking can be detrimental to your financial wealth.

20. Don't make investment or trading decisions based on tips. Tips are something you leave for good service.

21. Where there is smoke, there is fire, or there is never just one cockroach: In other words, bad news is usually not a one-time event; more usually follows.

22. Realize that a loss in the stock market is part of the investment process. The key is not letting it turn into a big one as this could devastate a portfolio. Said another way, "It's not the ones that you sell that keep going up that matter. It's the one that you don't sell that keeps going down that does."

Table 10.1 depicts the percentage gain necessary to get back even, after a certain percentage loss.

TABLE 10.1
Investment Return Required to Recover Investment Loss
(in percentage)

Percent Loss	Percent Gain
−5%	5.26%
−10%	11.11%
−15%	17.65%
−20%	25.00%
−25%	33.33%
−30%	42.86%
−35%	53.85%
−40%	66.67%
−45%	81.82%
−50%	100.00%
−55%	122.22%
−60%	150.00%
−65%	185.71%
−70%	233.33%
−75%	300.00%
−80%	400.00%

Percent Loss	Percent Gain
−85%	566.67%
−90%	900.00%
−95%	1,900.00%

23. Your odds of success improve when you buy stocks when the technical pattern confirms the fundamental opinion.

24. *As many participants have come to realize from 1999 to 2010, during which the S&P 500 has made no upside progress, you can lose money even in the "best companies" if your timing is wrong. Yet, if the technical pattern dictates, you can make money on a short-term basis even in stocks that have a "mixed" fundamental opinion.*

25. *To the best of your ability, try to keep your priorities in line. Don't let the "greed factor" that Wall Street can generate outweigh other just as important areas of your life. Balance the physical, mental, spiritual, relational, and financial needs of life.*

26. Technical analysis is a windsock, not a crystal ball. It is a skill that improves with experience and study. Always be a student; there is always someone smarter than you!

The fifth and last trader, James Montier, is the author best known for his work on behavioural investing. His most recent book before becoming an asset manager in 2010 was *The Little Book of Behavioral Investing: How Not to Be Your Own Worst Enemy*. More recently, in his May 24, 2015, article for the *Telegraph*, "How to Invest in a Central Bank–Sponsored Speculative Bubble," James Montier gave his ideas on how to invest in the current zero interest rate environment. His advice: "Retail investors are free to hold as much cash as they like. The greatest challenge for retail investors is remaining patient in the current market while asset prices rise, but then again that is the difference between investing and speculation."

1. Always insist on a margin of safety.
2. *This time is never different.*

3. *Be patient and wait for the fat pitch.*
4. Be contrarian.
5. Risk is the permanent loss of capital, never a number.
6. Be leery of leverage.
7. *Never invest in something you don't understand.*

Humans are funny creatures. Although our parents, educators, mentors, and peers attempt to teach us by sharing their knowledge, we usually choose not to take their advice. Instead, we have to try new experiences ourselves and learn by making our own mistakes. Investors usually learn the same way, by trial and error. We call this "reinventing the wheel." However, there is one big difference in investing, and that is money. Because money is not unlimited, taking this advice and using it will save you considerable grief, not to mention save you from losing large amounts of your hard-earned cash. Not following these rules will most likely lead to heavy losses. For your convenience I have compiled a list of twelve golden rules derived from the advice of the experts. For your own sake, write them down and put them somewhere where they can be referred to at all times.

1. Patience is unconditional when investing.
2. There is no substitute for hard work.
3. Never average down (commit more capital to losing trades).
4. Never buy on inside information or tips.
5. You will never be right all the time.
6. Take losses quickly.
7. Better to know a few stocks well than little of many.
8. Understanding investor psychology is as important as fundamental and technical analysis.
9. Learn from your mistakes.
10. Never fall in love with a stock.
11. Human emotion is a big enemy.
12. Never invest in something you don't understand.
    Source: Realinvestmentadvice.com

CONCLUSION

There have been a couple of events that have had a profound effect on my life. The day I became a father is one. The second was a day like no other. There wasn't a cloud in the sky and the sun was glimmering off Lake Ontario. If you looked closely you could see across to the United States. It was a beautiful fall morning as I sat on the fifty-third floor of Scotia Plaza. I had just returned from a summer vacation touring Europe, something I had wanted to do since graduating from the University of Waterloo.

It was about 8:55 in the morning when I picked up the phone. It was my mother, of all people.

"Did you see what just happened?" she asked.

It was the morning of September 11, 2001.

I shared the office with my business partner and a great group of rookies, and we had a television on, but we kept the volume muted so we could discuss the market. I quickly leaped up to crank the volume and turn the channel to CNN, where they had just started coverage. I remember they weren't providing a lot of detail at first as to what kind of aircraft it was. Our first thought was that some disgruntled pilot had plowed a Cessna into one of the towers.

My business partner, who had spent some time going to school in the United States, instantly knew who the likely culprit was — Osama Bin Laden. He remembered when the World Trade Center was first attacked in 1993.

I looked out over Lake Ontario to observe what I hadn't noticed before: a large number of commercial aircraft circling, looking, I can only guess, for a place to land. Without skipping a beat, my partner and I looked at each other and agreed to get the hell out of the building. Scotia Plaza was one of the tallest towers in downtown Toronto at the time. Later that day the downtown core was evacuated, a little too late if something were to have happened there.

That day changed my life forever. Up until that point, my entire focus had been on building my business and securing my financial future. After 9/11, my life as it was really didn't seem to make sense. It's like I had hit the reset button. My relationships with family and friends changed. Just as importantly, my relationships with clients changed. They became deeper, more meaningful, and more fulfilling.

I can truly say I love what I do for a living. I am passionate about being a financial advisor. I hope you enjoyed reading my book as much as I enjoyed writing it. I wish you success in making your dreams a reality by implementing the strategies I have shared with you. I hope in return you will share your success stories with me. Should you have any additional questions or if you would like to speak with me about creating your own Plan, I invite you to contact me. I would love to hear from you. Good luck! I wish you an abundance of health, happiness, and prosperity.

Yours truly,
Alan Dustin
alan@thenextbullmarket.com

APPENDIX

THE PLAN ALL-STAR TEAM

ALIMENTATION COUCHE-TARD INC. — CONSUMER STAPLES

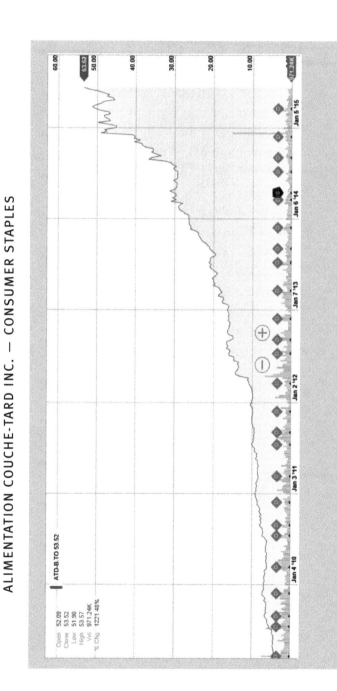

COMPANY INFORMATION	TSX-ATD.B www.couche-tard.com
	Couche-Tard is a leading convenience store operator with approximately 14,700 locations worldwide
	Yield 0.51%; Institutional ownership 26%
TARGET PRICE: $4.05	Price target is based on 2009 low of $4.05 adjusted for 3 for 1 split on April 23, 2014
SAFETY: B	Satisfactory balance sheet
	Debt rated as investment grade by S&P rating service
STRENGTHS	Excellent operator and proven ability to deleverage balance sheet
	Extensive product line of private-label brands
	Acquisition of 279 Esso gas stations from Imperial Oil increasing Ontario footprint
WEAKNESSES	Economic conditions, foreign exchange rates, interest rates, low fuel costs
OPPORTUNITIES	Fragmented market gives acquisition strategy enormous growth potential
	Growth in emerging economies where Couche-Tard has no presence
THREATS	Technology — shift to electric vehicles
	Restrictions on sale of tobacco products

Credit (graph): Yahoo! Finance

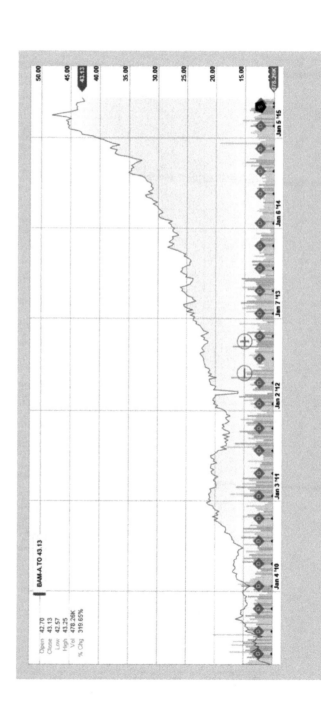

BROOKFIELD ASSET MANAGEMENT INC. — FINANCIALS

COMPANY INFORMATION	TSX-BAM.A www.brookfield.com
	Brookfield is a global alternative-asset manager with approximately $225 billion in assets under management
	Yield 1.11%; Institutional ownership 62%
TARGET PRICE: $10.28	Price target is based on 2009 low of $10.28 adjusted for 3 for 2 split on May 13, 2015
SAFETY: B+	Good balance sheet
	Debt rated as investment grade by S&P rating service
STRENGTHS	Financial strength will allow to thrive in adverse financial conditions
	Invests only in high-quality assets at mispriced levels in prime real estate locations
	Management strategy to increase fee-based revenue
WEAKNESSES	Real asset value price stability and capital market conditions
	Occupancy rates falling in event of global recession
OPPORTUNITIES	Financial strength allows for strategic acquisitions as opportunities arise
	Investment and growth in renewable energy sources
	Global operations with local personnel expertise
THREATS	Increasing interest rates remain an industry concern
	Susceptible to economic conditions

Credit (graph): Yahoo! Finance

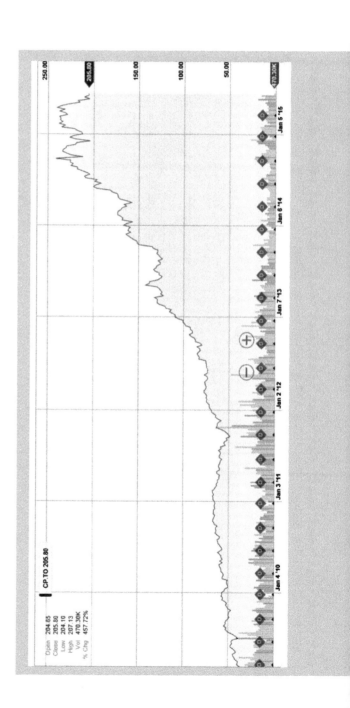

COMPANY INFORMATION	TSX-CP www.cpr.ca
	Canadian Pacific Railway is engaged in rail transportation
	Yield 0.68%; Institutional ownership 84%
TARGET PRICE: $36.90	Price target is based on 2009 low of $36.90
SAFETY: B+	Excellent balance sheet
STRENGTHS	CEO Hunter Harrison
	Operating efficiency ratio has been dramatically improved
	Increasing terminal efficiencies and technology
WEAKNESSES	Economic sensitivity to North American slowdown
	Limited access to U.S. routes that plays to the strength of
	Canadian National
	Pension liabilities
OPPORTUNITIES	Industry consolidation to enhance route flows and eliminate
	congestion
	Real estate portfolio used for potential development, lease, or sale
	Intermodal transport over trucking
THREATS	Low commodity prices will eventually begin to impact
	profitability
	Regulatory hurdles to industry consolidation

Credit (graph): Yahoo! Finance

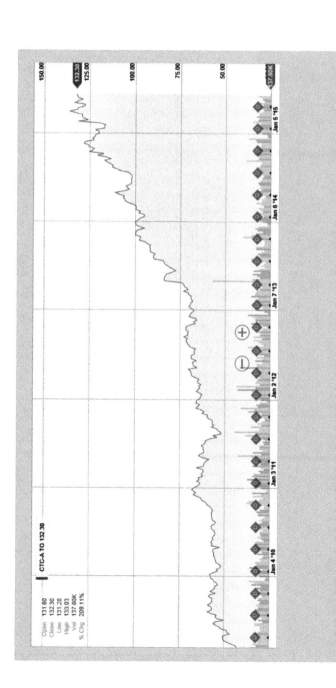

CANADIAN TIRE CORPORATION — CONSUMER DISCRETIONARY

COMPANY INFORMATION	TSX-CTC.A www.canadiantire.ca
	Canadian Tire is engaged in businesses that include a retail segment, a financial services division, and CT REIT
	Yield 1.59%; Institutional ownership 28%
TARGET PRICE: $42.80	Price target is based on 2009 low of $42.80
SAFETY: A	Excellent balance sheet
STRENGTHS	Unlocking real estate value in separate REIT
	Discounted gas outlets attract customers to store locations but lower gas prices reduce profits
WEAKNESSES	Retail space in Canada is challenging and extremely competitive (Sport Chek, Mark's)
	Geographically constrained to Canada
OPPORTUNITIES	Financial services loyalty programs and marketing initiatives add to growth
	Digitization of retailing using technology (online, internet)
THREATS	Decline in household spending due to weak economic conditions
	Increased costs due to foreign exchange rates and global sourcing of key products

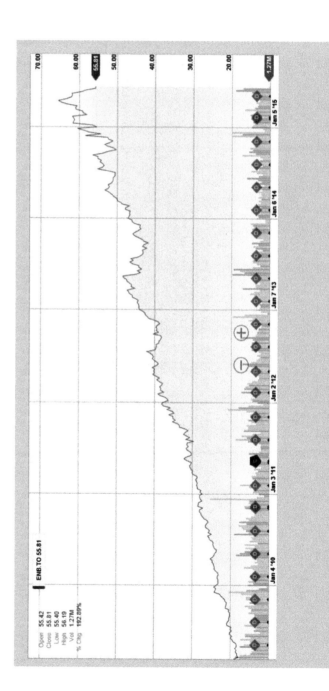

ENBRIDGE INC. — ENERGY

COMPANY INFORMATION	TSX-ENB www.enbridge.com
	Enbridge provides transportation and distribution of crude oil and natural gas
	Yield 3.80%; Institutional ownership 74%
TARGET PRICE: $19.06	Price target is based on 2009 low of $19.06 adjusted for 2 for 1 split on May 20, 2011
SAFETY: B+	Good balance sheet
STRENGTHS	Has longest crude oil and liquid pipeline system in the world
	Strategic management capability
	Increasing global energy demand
WEAKNESSES	High operational costs and aging infrastructure
	Spill and environmental violations have affected brand image
	Continued dependence on U.S. market and limited access to overseas markets
OPPORTUNITIES	Emphasis on renewable energy such as wind and solar
	Need for pipeline capacity in Canada
THREATS	Environmental agencies and interest groups
	Government regulation and opposition to pipeline construction in the United States

Credit (graph): Yahoo! Finance

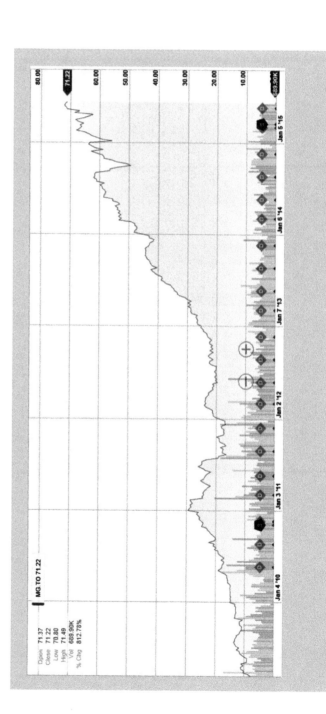

MAGNA INTERNATIONAL INC. — CONSUMER DISCRETIONARY

COMPANY INFORMATION	TSX-MG www.magna.com Magna is a leading global automotive parts supplier Yield 1.24%; Institutional ownership 75%
TARGET PRICE: $7.80	Price target is based on 2009 low of $7.80 adjusted for 2 for 1 split on Nov 12, 2010, and 2 for 1 split on March 26, 2015
SAFETY: A	Excellent balance sheet
STRENGTHS	More than 400 manufacturing and product development facilities in 29 countries Company has won a lot of "takeover" business from financially weaker sector players Strategic acquisitions of companies in markets underserved by Magna
WEAKNESSES	Top six clients represent 80% of sales
OPPORTUNITIES	Exposure to the Asia-Pacific region is still limited where Japanese auto makers are experiencing sales records Gas prices and borrowing costs remaining low for extended time period
THREATS	Peak auto sales Global economic weakness and threat of global recession

Credit (graph): Yahoo! Finance

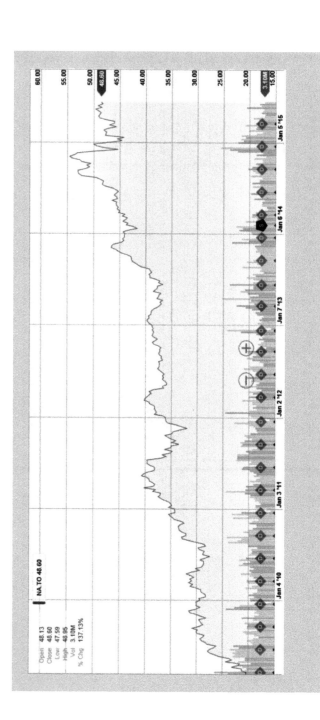

NATIONAL BANK — FINANCIALS

COMPANY INFORMATION	TSX-NA www.nbc.ca
	National Bank provides a full array of banking services
	including retail, corporate, and investment banking
	Yield 4.44%; Institutional ownership 27%
TARGET PRICE: $20.50	Price target is based on 2009 low of $20.50 adjusted for 2 for 1
	split on Feb 14, 2014
SAFETY: B+	Excellent balance sheet
STRENGTHS	Limited exposure in energy regions
	Good dividend yield for income-oriented investors
WEAKNESSES	Retail mortgage and HELOC portfolio is concentrated in
	Quebec at 63% and 22% in Ontario
	Limited number of physical branch locations
OPPORTUNITIES	Wealth management business has been consistently growing
	Opportunity to grow in other parts of Canada
THREATS	Proprietary trading

Credit (graph): Yahoo! Finance

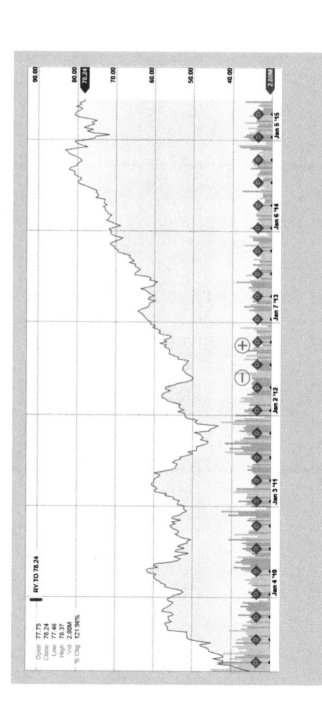

ROYAL BANK — FINANCIALS

COMPANY INFORMATION	TSX-RY www.rbc.com Royal Bank provides personal and commercial banking, wealth management services, insurance, corporate and investment banking Yield 4.04%; Institutional ownership 55%
TARGET PRICE: $35.25	Price target is based on 2009 low of $35.25
SAFETY: A	Excellent balance sheet
STRENGTHS	Growing global wealth management business Good dividend yield for income-oriented investors
WEAKNESSES	High consumer debt levels could slow down loan growth European sovereign debt crisis impacts credit markets
OPPORTUNITIES	Export of "Canadian Bank" image to other markets One of the largest global banks by market capitalization with operations in 39 countries
THREATS	Highest derivative exposure of all Canadian banks Weakness in U.S. economy and Canadian housing market Continued weakness in energy sector

Credit (graph): Yahoo! Finance

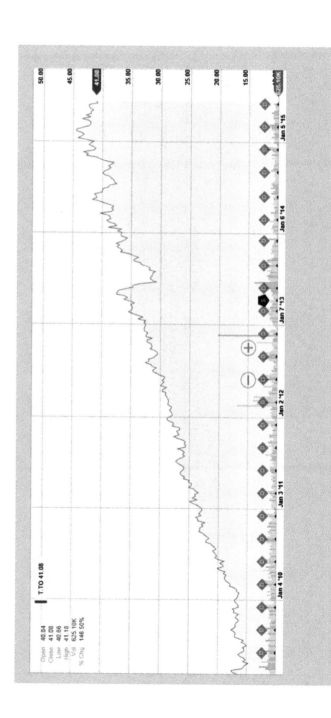

TELUS CORPORATION — TELECOMMUNICATIONS

COMPANY INFORMATION	TSX-T www.telus.com Telus provides telecommunications services and products including internet protocol, wireless, and data services Yield 4.28%; Institutional ownership 59%
TARGET PRICE: $16.67	Price target is based on 2009 low of $16.67 adjusted for 2 for 1 split on Apr 17, 2013
SAFETY: B+	Good balance sheet
STRENGTHS	Unique advertising and TV commercials make Telus a leading marketer Good dividend yield for income-oriented investors
WEAKNESSES	Smaller market share than Bell and Rogers Low store inventories may cause customers frustration and to look to competition
OPPORTUNITIES	Telus offers cable TV and internet service allowing for bundling discounts and cross-selling opportunities of existing customer base
THREATS	In a very competitive landscape and commoditized business pricing may be the only differentiator and directly impact profitability Reprogrammable eSIM cards

Credit (graph): Yahoo! Finance

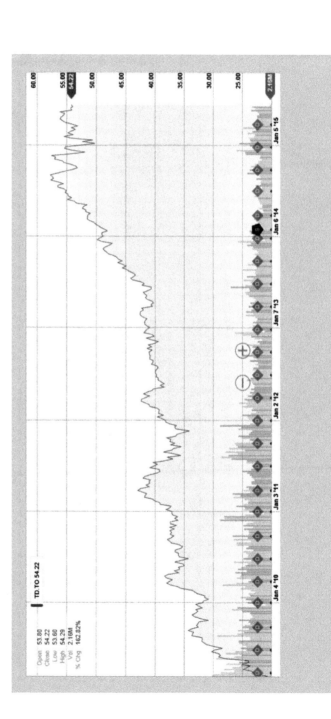

COMPANY INFORMATION	TSX-TD www.td.com TD Bank provides personal and commercial banking, wealth management, and insurance in Canada and the United States Yield 3.76%; Institutional ownership 62%
TARGET PRICE: $20.63	Price target is based on 2009 low of $20.63 adjusted for 2 for 1 split on Feb 3, 2014
SAFETY: B+	Excellent balance sheet
STRENGTHS	TD is a top ten bank in North America based on market capitalization and total assets 2,463 retail locations in North America with operations in 7 of 10 wealthiest states TD Meloche Monnex number one direct-to-consumer insurer
WEAKNESSES	High exposure to Canadian real estate market and commodity-based economy
OPPORTUNITIES	Comprehensive wealth offerings with significant opportunity to deepen relationships Primary issuer of Aeroplan Visa and acquisition of Chrysler auto financing TD Ameritrade and Epoch Investment Partners broaden asset management scope
THREATS	Slowing loan growth in Canada Low interest rates compressing net interest income Demanding regulatory environment

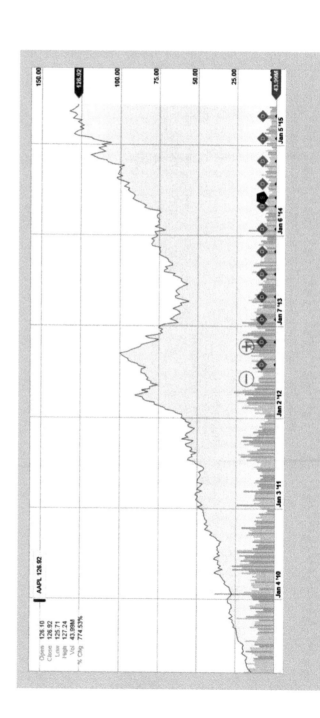

APPLE INC. — INFORMATION TECHNOLOGY

COMPANY INFORMATION	NASDAQ-AAPL www.apple.com Apple is one of the world's largest makers of PCs and peripheral and consumer products including the iPhone, iPad, and MacBook Yield 1.64%; Institutional ownership 60%
TARGET PRICE: $14.50	Price target is based on 2009 low of $14.50 adjusted for 7 for 1 split on June 9, 2014
SAFETY: A+	Excellent balance sheet Low level of debt
STRENGTHS	Brand loyalty and recognition worldwide iTunes and iCloud are a predictable source of recurring revenue
WEAKNESSES	Apple is up against the law of large numbers and growth may be slowing Potential tax liability of cash repatriation held outside the United States Security concerns
OPPORTUNITIES	What they plan to do with over $160 billion in cash Apple Watch, Apple TV, Apple Pay, Apple CarPlay
THREATS	Competitive threats from Alphabet, Facebook, and Microsoft who lead in cloud computing, virtual reality, and artificial intelligence

Credit (graph): Yahoo! Finance

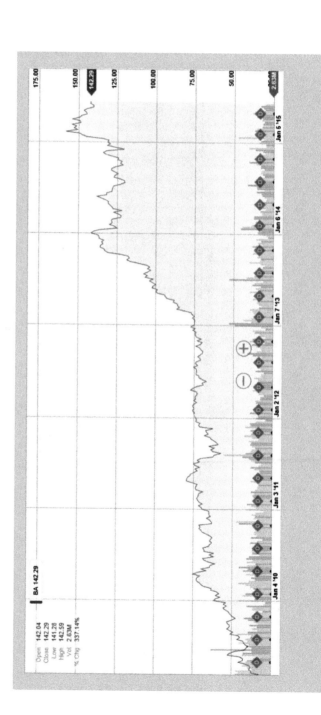

BOEING CO. — INDUSTRIALS

COMPANY INFORMATION	NYSE-BA www.boeing.com
	The Boeing Company is a leading manufacturer of commercial aircraft
	Yield 3.06%; Institutional ownership 76%
TARGET PRICE: $32.55	Price target is based on 2009 low of $32.55
SAFETY: A+	Excellent balance sheet
STRENGTHS	Best-in-class manufacturer and developer of fuel efficient and state of the art commercial and military aircraft
WEAKNESSES	General conditions in the economy
	High research and development spending
	Pension liabilities
OPPORTUNITIES	International defence-growth opportunities
	Robust commercial order book backlog including 787 Dreamliner
THREATS	Competition from Airbus and Embraer
	U.S. government defence spending and budgets

Credit (graph): Yahoo! Finance

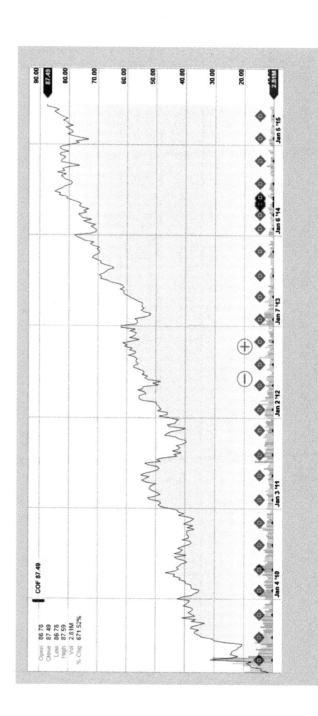

CAPITAL ONE FINANCIAL CORP. — FINANCIALS

COMPANY INFORMATION	NYSE-COF www.capitalone.com Capital One is one of the largest providers of MasterCard and Visa credit cards in North America and offers other consumer lending and deposit services Yield 1.83%; Institutional ownership 90%
TARGET PRICE: $11.34	Price target is based on 2009 low of $11.34
SAFETY: A	Excellent balance sheet
STRENGTHS	Use of loyalty reward programs and incentives increase card usage and profitability Capital One is extremely diligent at collecting outstanding loans Early adaptors and creators of technology
WEAKNESSES	Government regulation and restrictions on fees charged Interchange fee compression due to merchant reluctance and available alternatives
OPPORTUNITIES	Won Costco co-brand business from American Express in Canada Acquisition of Hudson's Bay Saks Five Avenue credit card business Auto financing and commercial banking business providing good growth
THREATS	American Express, Discover, bank-issued Visa and MasterCard, debit, PayPal, new technology eliminating need for centralized third party such as blockchains, M-Pesa, and cryptocurrencies

Credit (graph): Yahoo! Finance

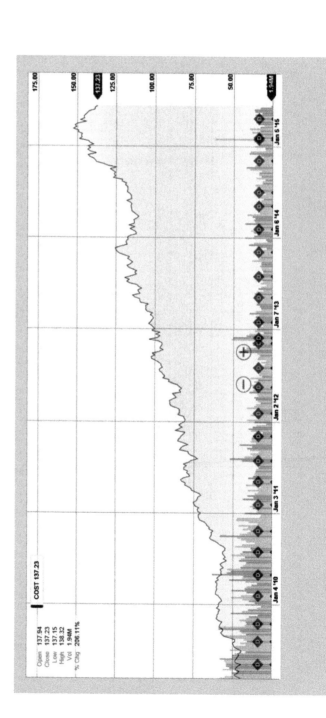

COSTCO WHOLESALE CORP. – CONSUMER STAPLES

COMPANY INFORMATION	NASDAQ-COST www.costco.com
	Costco operates wholesale-membership warehouses worldwide
	Yield 1.17%; Institutional ownership 72%
TARGET PRICE: $44.83	Price target is based on 2009 low of $44.83
SAFETY: A+	Excellent balance sheet
STRENGTHS	Quality goods at most competitive prices
	Discounted gas sales are low margin but attract customers to locations
	Food court sales are low margin but keep customers in the store longer
WEAKNESSES	Membership fees are 75% of earnings and are almost all profit
	Not doing a good job at attracting millennials that tend to live in urban areas
	Employees are paid substantially more than minimum wage
OPPORTUNITIES	Online e-commerce is very small percentage of sales
	New warehouses and conversion to executive memberships
THREATS	Walmart, Amazon, or other big box retailers
	Renewal subscriptions are at 91%
	Older customer base

Credit (graph): Yahoo! Finance

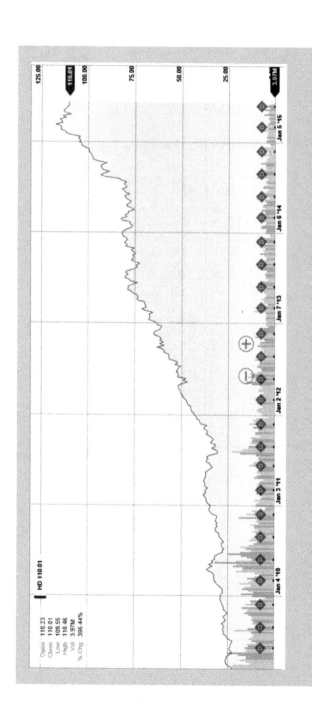

THE HOME DEPOT INC. — CONSUMER DISCRETIONARY

COMPANY INFORMATION	NYSE-HD www.homedepot.com The Home Depot operates a chain of 2,273 retail building supply/home improvement warehouse stores across the U.S., Canada, and Mexico Yield 2.15%; Institutional ownership 73%
TARGET PRICE $22.16	Price target is based on 2009 low of $22.16
SAFETY A+	Excellent balance sheet Has a considerable amount of debt
STRENGTHS	Built great relationships with professional contractors Equipment rental is a growing segment of business Diversified product mix
WEAKNESSES	Completely dependent on the Americas and economic cycle Concerns of associate disinterest and poor customer service
OPPORTUNITIES	Online e-commerce and home delivery convenience will be a long-term growth driver Global expansion in South America and Asia
THREATS	Lowe's, Walmart, and other niche appliance and construction suppliers

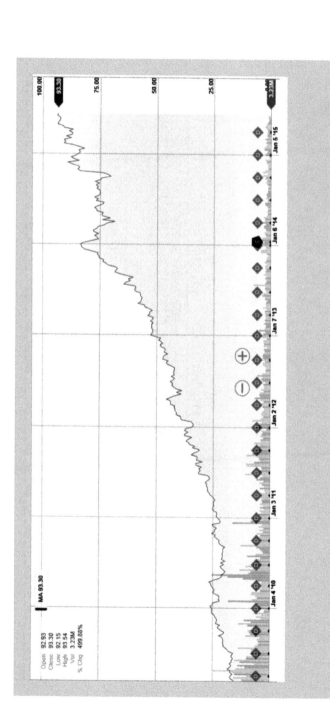

MASTERCARD INC. — INFORMATION TECHNOLOGY

COMPANY INFORMATION	NYSE-MA www.mastercard.com MasterCard is a global leader in electronic payments Yield 0.81%; Institutional ownership 78%
TARGET PRICE: $15.55	Price target is based on 2009 low of $15.55 adjusted for 10 for 1 split on Jan 22, 2014
SAFETY: A+	Excellent balance sheet
STRENGTHS	Strong brand recognition "Priceless" marketing campaign is innovative and consumer oriented
WEAKNESSES	Government regulation and restrictions on fees charged Interchange fee reduction due to Merchant reluctance and available alternatives
OPPORTUNITIES	Authentication using facial recognition Shift to cashless society
THREATS	Visa, American Express, debit, PayPal, new technology eliminating need for centralized third party such as blockchains, M-Pesa, and cryptocurrencies

Credit (graph): Yahoo! Finance

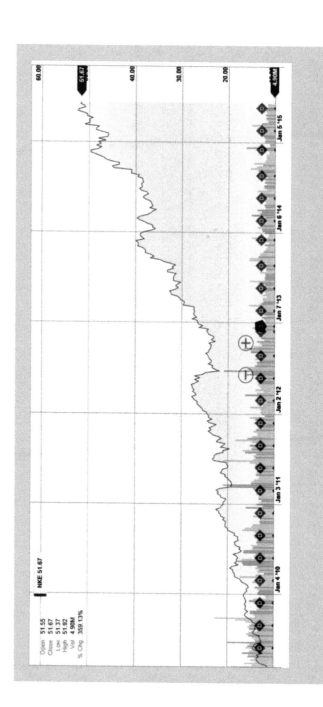

NIKE INC. — CONSUMER DISCRETIONARY

COMPANY INFORMATION	NYSE-NKE www.nikeinc.com Nike designs, develops, and markets footwear, apparel, equipment, and accessories Yield 1.24%; Institutional ownership 82%
TARGET PRICE: $11.26	Price target is based on 2009 low of $11.26 adjusted for 2 for 1 split on Dec 26, 2012
SAFETY: A+	Excellent balance sheet
STRENGTHS	Brand recognition, marketing savvy Research and development of innovative products Commands largest share of the global sportswear market at 16%, Adidas at 11%
WEAKNESSES	Unable to sign best athletes to brand due to better incentives from competition Inability to find replacement for Phil Knight, Nike's founder and chair to retire Poor labour practices
OPPORTUNITIES	Nike has the means to pay athletes top dollars for endorsements Michael Jordan Brand shoes brought in over $2 billion for Nike in fiscal 2015 Increasing market share in emerging markets such as China
THREATS	Largest competitive threats are Under Armour and Adidas Currency exchange rate volatility

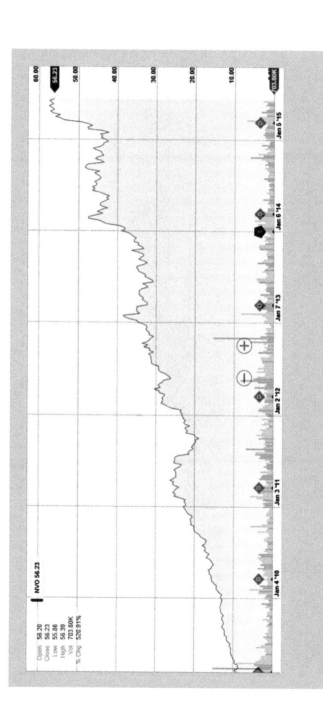

NOVO NORDISK — HEALTH CARE

Concept (Mark with an "X")	Form number
Entry ☐ Departure ☐	

IMPORTANT: Fill only one form per family unit when declaring cash or monetary instrument

Traveler information

Type of Identification Document: Col. Citizenship Card ☐ Passport ☐ Identification Number

Col. Identification Card ☐ Col. Alien Card ☐ Other ☐

First family name	Second family name	First given name	Other given names

Address in Colombia	City

Travel information

Mode of transport: Sea ☐ Land ☐ Air ☐	Carrier's name	Flight No. / Voyage No. / Vehicle No.

Do you reside in Colombia? Yes ☐ No ☐	If NOT a Colombian resident, Country of residence	How many days will you stay in Colombia or have you stayed abroad?

Not including tickets or tourist package, what will be (or were) your expenses during the trip? USD	If your expenses include those of your family unit, indicate the number of people with which you shared (will share) expenses

	Yes	No
Does all your luggage arrive or leave with you?	☐	☐
Are you carrying within your luggage goods other than personal effects valued in excess of $1.500 USD?	☐	☐
Are you temporarily bringing goods other than your personal effects into or out of the country?	☐	☐
Do you carry Colombian national heritage goods or national heritage goods of other nations?	☐	☐
Do you carry animals, plants or goods of animal or plant origin?	☐	☐
Do you or does the family unit traveling with you carry currency or cash in Colombian legal currency in excess of $10.000 USD or its equivalent in foreign currency?	☐	☐
Do you or does the family unit traveling with you carry monetary instruments or Colombian legal currency in excess of $10.000 USD or its equivalent in foreign currency?	☐	☐

If you have answered any of the last six questions affirmatively, please list the goods, cash, or monetary instruments

Declared cash or monetary instruments

Item	Type (cash or monetary instrument)	Currency	Value
1			
2			

Are you acting on behalf of a third party? Yes ☐ No ☐

Luggage information

Item	Quantity	Goods description (Brand, model, serial number)	Temporary entry or exit	USD Value	Customs value (Official use only)
1					
2					
3					
			Total value in USD		

If the space provided is insufficient, or if you need a duplicate of this declaration, please use an additional form, indicating herein the corresponding "Form number"

Traveler's signature	Date of arrival / departure
	Year Month Day

2015934 10317194

Assessment of duties	
Exchange rate	Tax base
Applicable rate **15%**	Single duty value in pesos
For official use only	
Official's signature	Name Position

General Information

All travelers entering or leaving Colombia must complete this form. Subject to this obligation, singly duty exempt goods brought within accompanied luggage and valued at fifteen hundred US Dollars ($1.500 USD) or less, or its equivalent in foreign currency, are excepted from being declared in this form.

Travelers or family units bringing into or out of the country cash and/ or monetary instruments in excess of ten thousand US Dollars ($10.000 USD) or its equivalent in foreign currency, must declare in only one 530 Form, the total amount brought in or out.

The amount of ten thousand US Dollars ($10.000 USD), or its equivalent in foreign currency, is applied independently and autonomously to cash and monetary instruments.

I. Cash or monetary instruments brought into or out of the country.

1. Cash brought into or out of the country. In this form, you as a traveler must declare before the Colombian customs authority the cash you are bringing into or out of the country, when the corresponding amount is in excess of ten thousand US Dollars ($10.000 USD), or its equivalent in foreign currency. Failure to do so will result in the amount in excess being withheld by the customs authority. If the cash brought into or out of the country by the traveler or his family unit is not in excess of ten thousand US Dollars ($10.000 USD), it does not need to be declared in this form.

2. Monetary instruments brought into or out of the country. Monetary instruments include checks, money orders, and any other document that serves a function identical to cash in the payment of liabilities. In this form, you as a traveler must declare before the Colombian customs authority the monetary instruments you are bringing into or out of the country, when the corresponding amount is in excess of ten thousand US Dollars ($10.000 USD), or its equivalent in foreign currency. In this form you must indicate the type of instrument (check, money order, etc.), currency (USD, Euro, Pound, etc.), and value, indicating whether in this operation you are acting on behalf of a third party.

II. Entry and exit of goods.

All travelers entering Colombia may bring as luggage their personal effects (new or used items needed for personal use throughout the trip, but not including commercial merchandise), as well as goods for personal or family use, household items, sporting goods and goods pertaining to the traveler's art, profession, or trade, subject to the following conditions and quotas:

Days spent abroad	Maximum USD quota	Tipo de Bienes	Maximum quantity	Duty	Type of luggage
Any length of time	$1.500 USD	Personal and / or family use	Non-commercial quantities	Duty-free	Luggage arriving with the traveler
Five (5) or more days	$2.500 USD	Household items, sporting goods; goods pertaining to the traveler's art, profession or trade	Three (3) of each	15% for single tax	Luggage arriving before, after, or with the traveler

The indicated quotas are annual and personal. Minors are allowed 50% of the quota.

Travelers may not bring as luggage, goods such as: tires, automobile spare parts, guns, ammunition or explosives.

Temporary entry of goods. A traveler residing abroad may temporarily enter, on a duty-free basis, items for personal or professional use or goods used during his stay in Colombia, and may declare them in this form. Upon departure, these goods must be presented to customs.

Temporary exit of goods. When a traveler temporarily exits with goods other than personal effects within his luggage, seeking to reenter them to the country on a duty-free basis, the traveler must declare said goods in this form upon departure.

National heritage goods of Colombia or other nations. A traveler must declare in this if he is entering or exiting the country with heritage goods or goods of cultural interest of Colombia or other nations.

Goods of animal or plant origin. A traveler must declare in this form if he is entering or exiting the country with animals, plants, or goods of animal or plant origin.

Warning

Failure to declare cash or monetary instruments brought into or out of the country, or declaring false, incomplete, or incorrect data, may lead to penalties and the cash and monetary instruments being withheld by the customs authority.

If the traveler declares his luggage, and the customs authority detects that it contains goods other than authorized goods, or that the goods do not meet the conditions or minimum time requirements abroad, the goods shall be sent to a warehouse and subjected to ordinary importation.

If the traveler fails to declare goods subject to the single duty, or goods exceeding the allowable limits in value or quantity within the luggage, or goods other than those authorized for travelers or that do not meet the minimum time requirements abroad, and the customs authority detects it, the goods shall be seized and confiscated.

COMPANY INFORMATION	NYSE-NVO (ADR) www.novonordisk.com
	Novo Nordisk is a major producer of insulin and diabetes-care products
	Yield 1.30%; Institutional ownership 37%
TARGET PRICE: $9.06	Price target is based on 2009 low of $9.06 adjusted for 5 for 1 split on Jan 9, 2014
SAFETY: A+	Excellent balance sheet and financial ratios
STRENGTHS	Largest insulin manufacturer and innovative product developer
	Growth in obesity and an aging population
	Annual earnings growth averaging in excess of 20%
WEAKNESSES	Only a small percent of shares are held by institutions
	Lacks diversification in drug pipeline of which 80% of revenue is insulin
OPPORTUNITIES	422 million people have diabetes worldwide and numbers continue to grow
	High barriers to entry
	Subsidies for diabetes medication
THREATS	Biggest competitive threats are Sanofi-Aventis and Eli Lilly
	Regulatory agencies prevent new drug approval

Credit (graph): Yahoo! Finance

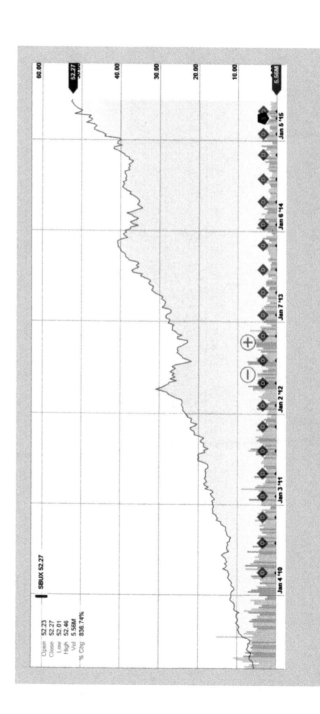

STARBUCKS CORPORATION — CONSUMER DISCRETIONARY

COMPANY INFORMATION	NASDAQ-SBUX www.starbucks.com
	Starbucks is the leading retailer, roaster, and brand of specialty coffee in the world
	Yield 1.53%; Institutional ownership 71%
TARGET PRICE: $5.58	Price target is based on 2009 low of $5.58 adjusted for 2 for 1 split on April 9, 2015
SAFETY: A	Excellent balance sheet
STRENGTHS	Powerful brand recognition and loyalty reward program
	Innovator in specialty product creation and mobile payment methods
	Breakfast, lunch, and snacks expanding the appeal of many of the 22,500 stores
WEAKNESSES	Inability to find replacement for CEO Howard Schultz
	Stock always trades at premium price earnings multiple
OPPORTUNITIES	Introduction of beer and wine and selected stores
	Plans to double footprint in China and Asia-Pacific region in five years
	Starbucks Express kiosks at high traffic locations
THREATS	Competition from McDonald's and saturation in available markets

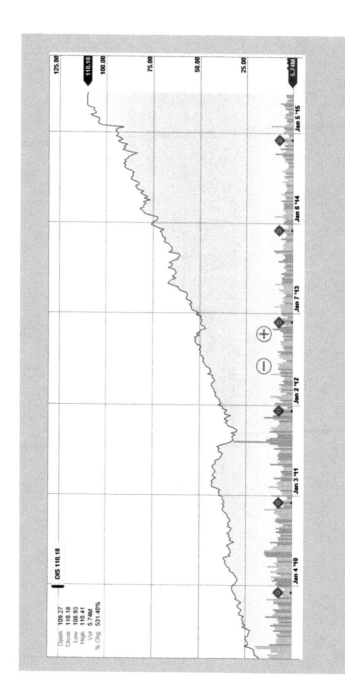

WALT DISNEY CO. — CONSUMER DISCRETIONARY

COMPANY INFORMATION	NYSE-DIS www.thewaltdisneycompany.com
	Disney operates media networks including ESPN, theme parks, cruise lines, and movie production and distribution (Pixar, Marvel, Lucasfilm)
	Yield 1.29%; Institutional ownership 61%
TARGET PRICE: $17.45	Price target is based on 2009 low of $17.45
SAFETY: A	Excellent balance sheet
STRENGTHS	Brand recognition
	Blockbuster movie franchises such as *Star Wars* and *Frozen* with merchandizing
WEAKNESSES	ESPN subscriptions decreasing
OPPORTUNITIES	Content creator may initiate new digital distribution deals or acquire streaming service
	Demand-based ticket pricing for U.S. theme parks
THREATS	Netflix, online streaming services

Credit (graph): Yahoo! Finance

RECOMMENDED READING

Chicago Board Options Exchange. *Options: Essential Concepts and Trading Strategies.* 3rd ed. New York: McGraw-Hill, 1999.

Cramer, James J. *Confessions of a Street Addict.* New York: Simon & Schuster, 2002.

Engel, Louis, and Brendan Boyd. *How to Buy Stocks.* 7th ed. New York: Bantam, 1987.

Ferguson, Niall. *Civilization: The West and the Rest.* Toronto: Penguin, 2011.

Galbraith, John Kenneth. *The Great Crash 1929.* Boston: Mariner, 2009.

Gladwell, Malcolm. *Blink: The Power of Thinking Without Thinking.* New York: Little, Brown and Company, 2007.

———. *Outliers: The Story of Success.* New York: Little, Brown and Company, 2008.

———. *The Tipping Point: How Little Things Can Make a Big Difference.* New York: Little, Brown and Company, 2006.

Gluskin, Alexander M. *Confessions of an Options Strategist.* Toronto: Hounslow, 1985.

Graham, Benjamin. *The Intelligent Investor.* New York: HarperCollins, 2006.

Graham, Benjamin, and David L. Dodd. *Security Analysis.* 6th ed. New York: McGraw-Hill, 2008.

Iacocca, Lee, and William Novak. *Iacocca.* New York: Bantam, 2007.

Kahneman, Daniel. *Thinking Fast and Slow*. Toronto: Anchor Canada, 2013.

Lefèvre, Edwin. *Reminiscences of a Stock Operator*. Hoboken, NJ: John Wiley & Sons, 2005.

Lewis, Michael. *The Big Short*. New York: W.W. Norton & Company, 2010.

———. *Liar's Poker*. New York: W.W. Norton & Company, 2014.

Livio, Mario. *The Golden Ratio*. New York: Broadway Books, 2008.

McMillan, Lawrence G. *Options as a Strategic Investment*. Upper Saddle River, NJ: Prentice Hall Press, 2012.

Naisbitt, John. *Megatrends: Ten New Directions Transforming Our Lives*. New York: Grand Central, 1988.

Partnoy, Frank. *F.I.A.S.C.O.: Blood in the Water on Wall Street*. New York: W.W. Norton & Company, 2010.

Rickards, James. *The Death of Money: The Coming Collapse of the International Monetary System*. New York: Portfolio, 2014.

Schwager, Jack D. *Hedge Fund Market Wizards: How Winning Traders Win*. Hoboken, NJ: John Wiley & Sons, 2012.

———. *Market Wizards: Interviews with Top Traders*. Hoboken, NJ: John Wiley & Sons, 2012.

———. *The New Market Wizards: Conversations with America's Top Traders*. New York: HarperCollins, 2009.

———. *Stock Market Wizards: Interviews with America's Top Stock Traders*. New York: HarperCollins, 2009.

Stewart, James B. *Den of Thieves*. 2012. New York: Simon & Schuster, 1992.

Taleb, Nassim Nicholas. *The Black Swan: The Impact of the Highly Improbable*. 2nd ed. New York: Random House, 2010.

Trump, Donald J., and Tony Schwartz. *Trump: The Art of the Deal*. New York: Ballantine, 2009.

Zweig, Martin. *Winning on Wall Street*. New York: Grand Central, 2009.

GLOSSARY

asset allocation   a strategy that determines the weighting of different asset classes (cash, fixed income, and equity) held in an investment portfolio.

at the money   a call or put option whose strike price is equal to the underlying security's current market price.

balance of payments   the record of a country's importing, exporting, borrowing, and lending activities.

bear market   a period in which stock prices are falling by 20 percent or more.

bull market   an advancing market in which prices are increasing for a sustained period of time.

call option   an agreement that gives the holder the right to buy a security at a specific price and allows an investor to participate in the appreciation of an underlying asset for a fraction of its cost.

Canada Pension Plan (CPP)   a government pension plan to which all working Canadians contribute during their lifetime. Canadians draw on their pensions starting at age sixty to receive reduced benefits, age sixty-five to receive full benefits, or later to receive additional benefits.

cash any asset that is principal-guaranteed, including cash, money market instruments, treasury bills, redeemable GICs, or any other liquid asset that has no risk to loss of principal.

cash account a non-registered investment account in which you cannot borrow against the assets held.

central bank a government institution — such as the U.S. Federal Reserve, the European Central Bank, and the Bank of Canada — that controls a country or economic unit's monetary policy and works to maintain financial stability.

congested market also known as a consolidating market; a market typically characterized by the absence of a trend, consisting of short-lived up-and-down fluctuations in price (whipsaw action).

cost of carry the costs associated with holding an investment position, such as interest on borrowing and storage fees for physical assets.

counter-party risk the danger that the counter-party guaranteeing the other side of a transaction may suffer losses so significant that it is no longer able to meet its obligations.

cyclic market also known as a trading range market; a market that oscillates with shorter bull and bear movements within a trading range or that exists within a larger trend of a bull or bear market.

cyclical unemployment unemployment that is caused by the extremes of a recession or during an extended expansion.

defined benefit pension plan a pension plan funded by an employer.

defined contribution pension plan	a pension plan funded by an employee's contributions.
derivative	an instrument whose value is derived by a change in the price of an underlying asset.
duration	a bond price's sensitivity to interest rate changes.
equity	as an asset class, in common stocks, either public (traded on a stock exchange) or private (not traded on an exchange); in real estate, the difference between the value of a property and the amount remaining in the owner's mortgage on the property.
exchange-traded fund (ETF)	a low-cost alternative to mutual funds that replicates an index fund and trades like a stock.
fixed income	long-term debt instruments (maturing in more than three years), such as government and corporate bonds.
gig economy	the increasing reliance on part-time and contract workers to fill companies' labour needs.
hedging	using derivatives, taking a position that is opposite to or different from the primary position in order to mitigate or reduce risk exposure.
home equity line of credit (HELOC)	a line of credit taken out against the equity value of a property.
in the money	an option that is exercisable; the strike price of a call option is below the underlying security's current market price, or the strike price of a put option is above the security's market price.
index	a portfolio of securities that is tracked and considered representative of the market or a specific portion of it.

inflection point the point at which a security's or index's price trend changes direction in response to an event.

insured annuity an insurance product that provides a tax-efficient stream of income for a set period or for life; if the latter, upon the holder's passing, it provides beneficiaries with the capital initially placed in the policy.

Keynesian economics an economic theory that advocates state intervention to moderate the boom and bust cycles of economic activity.

limit order an order to buy a security up to a certain price but no higher, or an order to sell a security down to a certain price but no lower.

margin account an investment account in which you can borrow against the assets held, up to a certain percentage of their value (the margin).

market order an order to buy or sell a security at the current market price when the trade is executed.

negative interest rate policy (NIRP) a monetary policy through which a central bank sets its target interest rate below zero.

Old Age Security (OAS) a government pension plan that is funded out of Canada's general revenue and that pays a monthly benefit to Canadians aged sixty-five or older.

option a derivative product that represents the right to buy (call) or sell (put) a stock at a certain price.

out of the money an option that is not exercisable; the strike price of a call option is above the underlying security's current market price, or the strike price of a put option is below the security's market price.

put option	a derivative that gives the holder the right to sell a security at a certain price, protecting the value of an underlying asset against its potential loss.
retracement	a temporary reversal in the movement of a security's price that moves in a direction against the prevailing trend.
reverse mortgage	a mortgage borrowed against the value of a paid-for home. The home owner pays back the mortgage upon sale of the home or death.
short sale	the sale of a borrowed security with the expectation that the investor will be able to buy it back at a lower price and make money on the difference.
stop-loss order	an order to sell a stock when it reaches a certain price below its current market price to minimize loss.
strike price	the price at which a put or call becomes exercisable.
SWOT analysis	an analysis that identifies a company's strengths, weaknesses, opportunities, and threats.
systemic risk	the risk that a decision made by a company or government could spread to other companies or countries and result in the collapse of an entire system or market.
term to maturity	the amount of time left before a bond matures — either short-term (maturing in one to three years) or long-term (maturing in four or more years).
unemployment rate	the number of unemployed people, expressed as a percentage of the total of those who have jobs and those who are looking for them.

volatility   the degree to which a security deviates from its returns or those of the index; considered an indication of its risk.

yield   in fixed-income securities, the bond's interest rate as a percentage of its market price.

zero interest rate policy (ZIRP)   a monetary policy through which a central bank sets its target interest rate at zero.

ACKNOWLEDGEMENTS

I would like to thank a number of people at Dundurn for their hard work and contribution to the completion of this book. For starters, I want to thank Beth Bruder for giving me this wonderful opportunity. Dominic Farrell, words cannot express my gratitude for all of your dedication, guidance, and suggestions in transforming the manuscript from a collection of thoughts and ideas into coherent flowing prose. Kathryn Lane, your patience and understanding are recognized and appreciated.

Jenny Govier, your ability to interpret and express my thoughts in a simplistic and conversational manner was inspiring. Thank you so much. And finally, Anne Marie Kaye, I hope we can continue our friendship for many more years to come.

INDEX

ABOUT THE AUTHOR

Alan graduated from the University of Waterloo in 1990. Before becoming a financial advisor, he was an options specialist for one of Canada's leading discount brokerages. Alan has leveraged his unique understanding of derivatives to his clients' benefit ever since. In his spare time he has taught derivatives courses to industry professionals at the Canadian Securities Institute and Ryerson University. He has also instructed a professional financial planning course at George Brown College.

In addition, Alan specializes in a variety of financial subjects including retirement income solutions, family financial education, portfolio management, philanthropy, wealth accumulation, and estate preservation. Whether you are just starting to plan for your financial future or a seasoned investor, Alan has the knowledge, expertise, and past performance to guide you to a successful end result.

Alan has observed first-hand some extraordinary events during his career. In the late nineties, during the technology boom, Alan witnessed a co-worker take an advance of $6,000 on their credit card and in a few short years parlay that into $8 million. In the mid-2000s, a client of Alan's with a very modest income was able to accumulate a net worth of over $20 million in their lifetime. The principles and strategies employed by these two individuals to amass their fortunes are the same principles that are outlined in *How to Profit From the Next Bull Market*.

As an ongoing service to clients, readers of the book, and new subscribers, Alan provides updated commentary, research material, and investor tools free of charge to those who are serious about learning how to secure their financial futures. All of the material mentioned in the book including the two investment calculators, cashflow statements, loan payment calculator, and annual reports can be found at www.thenextbull market.com.

You can also visit the website to learn more about Alan, or contact him directly by emailing alanedustin@gmail.com or calling 416-319-2233. For Alan's insights on wealth building, personal finance, and the markets, follow him on Twitter (@NextBullMarket) or connect with him on Facebook (www.facebook.com/alan.dustin.39).

To download the tools and resources mentioned in this book go to
www.thenextbullmarket.com.